A THEOLOGY OF BROTHERHOOD

A Theology of Brotherhood

The Federal Council of Churches and the Problem of Race

Curtis J. Evans

NEW YORK UNIVERSITY PRESS
New York

NEW YORK UNIVERSITY PRESS
New York
www.nyupress.org

Please contact the Library of Congress for Cataloging-in-Publication data.
ISBN: 9781479820443 (hardback)
ISBN: 9781479820467 (library ebook)
ISBN: 9781479820450 (consumer ebook)

This book is printed on acid-free paper, and its binding materials are chosen for strength and durability. We strive to use environmentally responsible suppliers and materials to the greatest extent possible in publishing our books.

Manufactured in the United States of America

10 9 8 7 6 5 4 3 2 1

Also available as an ebook

CONTENTS

Introduction

On September 22, 1949, the Federal Council of the Churches of Christ in America (FCC) presented an amicus brief to the US Supreme Court on behalf of Heman Marion Sweatt in a case against the University of Texas Law School, which had denied him admission simply because he was Black. *Sweatt v. Painter*, decided in favor of Sweatt, would become a landmark case, later seen as chipping away at the separate but equal doctrine in the South. Charles H. Tuttle was the lawyer who represented the FCC as unpaid counsel. Tuttle had unsuccessfully run for governor of New York in 1930, as a Republican running against Democrat Franklin Delano Roosevelt. In 1944, he had served as counsel to the New York State Temporary Commission Against Discrimination, which drafted in 1945 a statute against discrimination in employment for reasons of race, creed, or national origin. Tuttle was an active member of the Episcopal Church, and had been a leader in the Greater New York Federation of Churches, and Brotherhood-in-Action, an interfaith group.[1] Clearly, he was ensconced in the upper echelons of the Protestant Establishment and brought cultural prestige to the FCC's racial work. In his brief for the FCC, he declared that segregation violated "the constitutional principles of equal protection under the law and also the free democratic principles and spiritual ideals which we profess as a nation." The amicus brief referred to the FCC's official position on segregation, articulated at a special meeting in Columbus, Ohio, in 1946, which asserted that it was a "denial of the equal protection of the laws, of the dignity and inherent rights of the individual human being and of the Christian concept of universal brotherhood."[2] The language of individual rights and the call for equal protection under the law were similar to that of the National Association for the

Advancement of Colored People (NAACP), which had brought this case before the Supreme Court, but what distinguished the FCC was its critique of segregation as a "violation of the Gospel of love and human brotherhood." The brief went on to call for a non-segregated church and society. The emphasis in this brief on Christian brotherhood as antithetical to southern segregation and white supremacy was a culmination of several decades of FCC racial work and theological reflection on the problem of racial division and oppression in the US and in Christian churches.

At its inception in 1908, the FCC defined its purpose in the following words: "to manifest the essential oneness of the Christian Churches of America in Jesus Christ as their Divine Lord and Saviour, and to promote the spirit of fellowship, service and cooperation among them."[3] Though the FCC, a precursor to today's National Council of Churches, had no authority to change church polity or dictate beliefs to local churches that formed this federation, it could "provide for a close and effective working together in order to secure larger combined influence for the Churches in matters affecting the religious and the moral and social condition of the people, so as to promote the application of the law of Christ in every relation of human life"[4] This foundational emphasis on uniting the churches around common causes, and bringing to bear their combined influences in all realms of life, would be the hallmark of the FCC's work for its more than four decades of existence (from 1908 to 1950). Its consistent focus on the essential oneness of churches and a spirit of fellowship, service, and cooperation would lead to the creation of its Commission on Negro Churches and Race Relations in 1921 (renamed the Commission on the Church and Race Relations by July 12 of that same year, and in 1932, when it became the Department of Race Relations). The principal goal of this department, to draw upon the wellsprings of the Christian tradition to try to solve the race problem in the United States, was an expression of a deep-seated concern that racially divided churches and racial oppression in the United States, a professed Christian nation, were serious obstacles to the witness and efficacy of the Christian faith.

The Federal Council of Churches was an interracial though largely white organization, but it was a progressive one. Comprised of various Protestant mainline denominations in the United States in the early twentieth century, it tended to embrace the Social Gospel, which pursued social justice issues from a Christian perspective. It was also concerned with issues including worker's rights, immigration, and equal rights for minority groups, though my focus is on their fight for African American rights. At the time in which it was active, what it said and did with regard to race relations and social reform was influential—as, indeed, mainline Protestantism more generally was the dominant religious force in the nation at this time. I argue that the Federal Council of Churches' Department of Race Relations was a crucial advocate for the dissemination of "progressive" views on race in the first half of the twentieth century. I make the case that the Federal Council of Churches' theological approach to race, and in particular its anti-lynching campaign—though that campaign failed to get Congress to act—were responsible in meaningful ways for progress in some white Protestant churches on racial issues.

With this book, I aim to add a missing voice to the huge literature on racism and anti-racism in the early twentieth century, which tends to highlight the work of the NAACP and other secular organizations. The FCC was a predominantly white, religious organization that in the early twentieth century contributed a distinctive and influential vision of racial and ethnic equality and worked for social and political reform. The FCC expanded and propagated a civic nationalist tradition that was grounded in a "universal brotherhood" and a belief in the equality of all human beings, over against a racial nationalist ideology that conceived of America in ethno-racial terms.

As I argue in this book, the FCC represents an important strand of ecumenical Christianity that has begun to receive scholarly reappraisal, especially within the last decade.[5] Older narratives on aspects of religion in the US, and most major survey texts (up to the 1970s) on American religious history, regarded the FCC as the institutional expression of Social Gospel Christianity. Now, the National Association of Evangelicals (NAE) and fundamentalist organizations are more likely to be mentioned than the FCC in surveys of the twentieth century. One reason for a decline of interest in religious organizations like the FCC is the rise of conservative Christianity since the 1970s and the almost total identification of Christian public and vocal stances on social issues with those of the Christian Right's leaders since the emergence of the Moral Majority in the 1980s.[6] Evangelical Protestants and conservative Christians have dominated most contemporary discussions of religion and public life. Yet the FCC's involvement in so many crucial social and political issues of the early twentieth century indicates that the relationship of Christian faith and public life is far richer than simply a story of the emergence of the Christian Right, important as that story is. Fortunately, a number of scholars have begun to reassess the historical and contemporary influence of the Protestant Left in its various forms. They are contributing to this broader narrative of publicly engaged liberal Protestant Christianity.[7]

Because it was part of the older Protestant Establishment or mainline Christianity, public knowledge of the FCC has seemingly declined in proportion to the decreasing influence of this segment of American Christianity.[8] Institutions and organizations came under great suspicion in the 1960s as the embodiment of suffocating and restrictive authority. Even later scholarship on the study of American religions seemed to follow this trend by paying little attention to institutional forms of Christianity. This kind of Christianity suffered the same fate as its own denominational histories. With good reason, many scholars were skeptical about the existing insider narratives of institutional history. They wanted to know what these histories left out about the ideas, practices, and trends beyond the singular details of a particular denomination or church. In view of this concern, I have sought to avoid a traditional institutional history that narrowly examines the internal dynamics and bureaucratic details of an organization. Rather, I focus on the projects that the FCC sponsored under its Department of Race Relations (and affiliated Departments) and how those projects differed, were similar to, and converged with other attempts at racial reform prior to the emergence of the Black freedom struggle of the 1950s. I situate the FCC within broader theological and sociological discussions of race in the first half of the twentieth century. By narrating one part of its institutional history, I show that the FCC contributed a distinctive religious element to efforts toward a pluralistic democracy, racial and ethnic diversity, and social and political reform. Broadly speaking, I provide a cultural and intellectual history of theological positions and moral ideas rather than the details of the institution, though I note the particulars of projects and institutional changes when they are illuminating and necessary to the story at hand.

In this book, I give special prominence to the FCC's Department of Race Relations and its foundational theology of brotherhood (the FCC had eight departments and a number of committees by the end of its existence in 1950). This theology undergirded its race relations project for three decades. The Department of Race Relations grounded its various programs, such as its anti-lynching campaign and its annual Race Relations Sundays, in this larger theological vision. I draw specific attention to the FCC's ecumenicity, a stream of Christianity that has emphasized, among other things, community, collaboration, universalism, and social justice. This ecumenical body urged churches to recognize and practice unity in the body of Christ by forging common theological bonds, cooperative mission work, and biblically and theologically grounded positions on social issues.[9] The theology of brotherhood was an outgrowth and implementation of the FCC's founding aims: expressing the fellowship and "catholic unity" of the Christian church and applying the "law of Christ in every relation of human life."[10] Although leaders of the FCC articulated a theology of brotherhood that was grounded in Scripture and the Christian tradition, they were much less inclined to quibble over detailed exegesis of various biblical passages and doctrinal "purity" than were their conservative counterparts, who showed almost no interest in or recognition of racial division and oppression.[11] The FCC's most commonly cited Scriptures were the following: Genesis 1:26–27 (humanity as image bearers and thus worthy of dignity, and an emphasis on the unity of human beings), Acts 17:26 (from one man or one blood, God created all human beings [a favorite text of abolitionists]), John 17 (Jesus' high priestly prayer for unity among his disciples), and Ephesians 2:11–19 (Jesus has broken down the wall of enmity between believers [Jews and Gentiles and, by extension, whites, Blacks, and other minority groups]). The theology of brotherhood was a serious challenge to the dominant theologies of segregation and white supremacy in that era. I explain the nature of those differences and the conflicts that resulted.

This theological vision of brotherhood and unity in the churches shaped the actual work and concrete projects of the Department of Race Relations and represented a break from the dominant scientific racism of the period and the theology of segregation that permeated most white southern churches. Though I give some attention to the details of the FCC's racial projects, especially when such information is available, there are inherent limitations in telling this kind of story. In many instances, the FCC incited or prompted action by local groups and watched (sometimes mostly giving advice) as the actual work progressed. For example, its extensive public relations campaign started as an educational resource that urged churches to act against lynching. The book's narrative focuses on the national organization as it operated out of New York City. The primary emphases are the FCC's distinctive theology of brotherhood and its official perspective and activity as a federation of churches whose ecumenical Christianity found America's racial oppression of Blacks to be contrary to the Christian gospel.

I define this theology of brotherhood as a positive affirmation of the unity of humanity, of the common bond of Christians in the body of Christ (which is the church), and of the fatherhood of God over all human beings.[12] It was a denial of invidious distinctions between the races, a repudiation of the hierarchical ordering of races, and a rejection of white supremacy purportedly grounded in the divine order. In practice, it urged Christian churches to fight against racial oppression within churches and in the broader society, to affirm their shared humanity and their common link to Christ as head of the church, and to welcome people of other races into their inner circles. Specifically, it meant the rejection of segregation, the right to vote for Black Americans, and the removal of discrimination from all aspects of American society. This emphasis on the civil and political rights of Blacks eventuated in a full-blown statement of human rights by 1949, which reaffirmed the FCC's 1946 Columbus, Ohio, non-segregation statement and called for the basic personal, social, economic, and political rights to which every individual is entitled "without discrimination as to race, sex, birth, social or economic status or creed."[13]

I have intentionally chosen the term "theology" to describe the beliefs and practices of the FCC because of their rootedness in Christian texts and traditions. The FCC was staffed by literate and highly educated leaders who attended seminaries, were involved in churches, and sought to elucidate from the Christian Scriptures the demands and requirements placed on modern Christians in the realm of racial and social reform. Some of these men and women had feet planted in both divinity/university contexts and in churches. They did not regard their work on the details of anti-lynching and civil rights as any less sacred than worship in a church or prayer on behalf of distressed neighbors.

I have historicized the emergence of this theology of brotherhood as a break from what historian Fay Botham calls a Protestant theology of race that originally emerged in the colonial period, when whites made slavery a perpetual, inheritable status for peoples of African descent. During the antebellum period, a southern version of this theology of race morphed into a theology of segregation, which argued that God created separate and hierarchical races with whites at the top.[14] Botham's longer history of a theology of race highlights significant debates about human origins, racial division and segregation, and the place of Blacks in the United States. The FCC's Department of Race Relations sought to confront and undermine this dominant theologizing about separate and inferior races.

The FCC's theology of brotherhood was a capacious vision of human unity that had specific relevance to the problems of racial division in the US, though it was never solely about the Black and white divide. By the time the FCC ended its tenure in 1950, it had actively engaged in work on behalf of Native Americans, Jewish Americans, Japanese Americans, Mexican Americans, African Americans, and other groups. It proffered a multi-racial and multi-cultural democracy, offering a vision in which each group would bring its distinctive gifts to enrich the nation as a whole. One segment of a radio script prepared by the FCC's Department of Race Relations stated in 1940: "Present day leaders are realizing that this old idea of Americanization [of all being fused into a single type] is unsound. In recent years there has developed a new idea of cultural democracy which points out that the quality of our civilization depends upon our ability to give to each other the best that we have in custom and tradition—and that differences when appreciated are elements of strength. The sharing of the valuable contributions of all groups will mean a richer culture than that of any one group."[15] This notion of "cultural gifts" set the FCC apart from the racial nationalism that vied with this more capacious civic vision.[16] It was also different from the growing social scientific consensus in the 1940s that African American culture was a pathological development that should be discarded in order to facilitate integration into the white mainstream. I have found no evidence that leaders of the FCC adopted wholesale the emerging paradigm of race relations put forward by Gunnar Myrdal's massive *American Dilemma* (1944), though they did agree with its indictment of American racism.[17] The FCC's cultural gifts model opposed an integrationist stance that presumed a one-sided model of Blacks assimilating into a white mainstream.

This book is a contribution to scholarship in three areas: visions of the American nation, religion and racial reform in the first half of the twentieth century, and the nature and fate of Social Gospel Christianity from the 1920s to the 1940s, particularly as the FCC represented the active persistence of the Social Gospel in this period. The FCC was deeply concerned about the American state, and its broader pluralist vision of brotherhood addressed questions of national unity, immigration policy, racial segregation, and the place and reputation of the US in the world.[18] Gary Gerstle's *American Crucible* (2001) argues that there have been two competing visions of the American nation: civic and racial nationalism. Civic nationalists held to a core of political ideals that included belief in the fundamental equality of all human beings; in every individual's inalienable right to life, liberty and the pursuit of happiness; and in a democratic government that derives its legitimacy from the people's consent. Competing with this vision was a racial nationalist ideology, which conceived of America in ethno-racial terms, as a people held together by common blood, skin color, and an alleged inherited fitness for self-government. This racial nationalism contained a yearning for America to be a white republic. It excluded Blacks, Asians, non-white Latin Americans, and, up the 1920s, southern and Eastern Europeans, as full-fledged citizens of the nation. Gerstle helpfully notes that both of these traditions were complex, simultaneously elastic and exclusionary (for example, even civic nationalists supported at times disciplinary measures with the aim of Americanizing immigrants). Neither was static, and thus the basis of exclusion and inclusion varied over time and in response to changing political and economic problems.[19]

Unlike Gerstle's work, which completely neglects religious traditions, I argue that Protestants in the FCC forwarded a civic nationalist vision that was grounded in "universal brotherhood," Christianity, democracy, and human liberty.[20] The FCC sought to contend with and reverse the racial or ethnic nationalism that was dominant at the turn of the century (and that experienced a new life in the 1920s). My focus is on a particular strand of Protestant Christianity as manifested in the FCC. I show that their theology of brotherhood contributed to and coincided with the civic nationalism that Gerstle depicts, and I highlight the contributions that a religious vision played in expanding and forwarding the civic nationalist tradition. Religion as a force for progressive social change and a critique of parochial or narrow racial categories is also a major theme of this narrative.

The book also takes a cue from Thomas J. Sugrue's massively researched *Sweet Land of Liberty: The Forgotten Struggle for Civil Rights in the North* (2008). Following historian Jacqueline Dowd Hall and others, Sugrue urges us to understand the Black freedom struggle as much broader than the events that took place in the South during the 1950s and 1960s, commonly understood as part of the "Civil Rights Movement." Rather, he argues that we need to go back further than most histories have, indeed as far back as the 1920s and 1930s, to understand more fully the nature of this struggle. Sugrue calls for a "long civil rights movement" historiography that attends to the creative strategies employed by Black and white activists to achieve racial equality.[21] He asks us to pay serious heed, for example, to the Protestant interracialism of the 1920s exhibited through the Young Men's Christian Association (YMCA) and the YWCA, the missionary movement, and the FCC. Although Sugrue asserts that the work of the FCC was often merely "symbolic" and committed to an ideal of persuasion, he also acknowledges that it attracted a number of activists who envisioned the problem of racial inequality as a moral problem. Sugrue writes, "Their vision of 'brotherhood,' that all were equal in the eyes of Christ, would lead a small but growing number of whites to embrace the goals of the fledgling struggle for Black equality."[22] It is precisely these activists whose words and works I examine in this book. I wrestle with implications of the extensive work of the FCC to bring about attitudinal and social change in a context in which moral suasion was the only tool available to it. The FCC rejected reliance on violence as an instrument of reform, which it felt violated the Christian gospel. There were few partners in government and political institutions to assist in their work to overturn racial oppression, and their anti-lynching campaign would in fact point out the severe limitations of direct appeal to the national Congress. The failure and refusal of Congress to pass a federal anti-lynching bill served as confirmation of the intractable forces of racial oppression, but also as further evidence for the need to change attitudes alongside applying political pressure and seeking federal legislation.

Previous scholarship that has discussed the various race projects of the FCC has been rather dismissive. As these historians have rightly noted, there were major limitations to and divided interests in the FCC's work to address racial oppression in the US. Even so, I offer a more charitable view based on a close reading of its rich archives, and I present a fuller discussion of the evolution of its racial work than previous studies. During their heyday, Race Relations Sundays in particular stood (in the eyes of detractors) as a symbol of the impotence and impracticality of the racial work in which the FCC engaged, especially prior to the emergence of a more active stance taken by the National Council of Churches in the 1960s. David Wills writes that Race Relations Sundays have always been an object of ridicule because of their emphasis on ritual and George Edmund Haynes's (who was their chief promoter as executive secretary of the Department of Race Relations) confidence in the "transformative power of positive interaction" and his belief that the universe was on the side of "human mutuality." Wills notes that, in the 1960s, Race Relations Sunday was widely criticized as a "trivial observance that treated a massive injustice as though it were a problem of disharmonious relations."[23] Yet, Wills does partially defend the work of Race Relations Sundays by noting that it was sufficiently provocative in the interwar years that Southern Presbyterians refused as late as 1935 to participate in it (a point that says more about Southern Presbyterians than it does about the FCC). He also points out that interracial reconciliation for Haynes was an end in itself, and a means to improve Black life in specific material ways. This is a crucial insight about what Haynes was seeking to accomplish through these events. As Wills rightly notes, Haynes did not simply rely on winning the goodwill of lynchers to stop lynching, but he lobbied energetically on behalf of federal anti-lynching legislation. Yet, Wills' rather weak attempt to defend Race Relations Sundays (and more generally the work of the entire Department) is another example of the skepticism with which they are regarded by scholars and detractors.

James Findlay's *Church People in the Struggle* (1993) offers a short and negative assessment of the Department of Race Relations, especially Race Relations Sundays. Findlay argues that the department's primary purpose was educational, which in his view was a shortcoming. Disseminating lots of information would presumably dispel prejudice. Mediation and conciliation, bringing Blacks and whites together for worship, fellowship, and face-to-face discussions—all of these tactics, he asserts, seem quite naïve to us today, especially in their cautious, evolutionary, go-slow approach to the solution of racial problems. These timid steps, Findlay maintains, were hardly going to change the "deeply rooted practices of racial discrimination in the United States."[24] The work of the Department of Race Relations, from its inception in 1921 to its conclusion in 1950, occupies less than two pages in Findlay's book. For him, it was only by the late 1950s that a real sense of crisis to act appeared, when frustration and moral impotence goaded the leaders of the newly incorporated National Council of Churches to rethink their mission and tactics. It was figures outside the NCC, especially African Americans like Martin Luther King, Jr., who were instrumental in prompting this sense of urgency.

Though not concerned with the FCC, David Chappell's *A Stone of Hope: Prophetic Religion and the Death of Jim Crow* (2004) does trace the antecedents of 1950s Civil Rights activism beginning his narrative with the work of secular white liberals in the 1930s, the period that coincides with the active racial projects of the FCC. Chappell argues that Black churches in the Civil Rights Movement supplied what these white liberals lacked. The success of the Civil Rights movement was based on a vital factor: religion, or what he calls "the irrational traditions of prophetic revivalistic religion."[25] Chappell's book not only raises problematic concern about his association of "emotional" religious traditions with Blacks over against the alleged sterility and passionless intellectualism of what he calls hungry white liberals (longing for this deep source of religious passion and basis for sacrifice), but the very intellectual genealogy that he provides, with John Dewey as a central figure, overlooks much of the theological foundation laid by organizations like the FCC. He rightly gives credit to Reinhold Niebuhr as a critic of the kinds of liberal Protestantism advocated by some in the FCC, though he fails to note Niebuhr's presence at and involvement in FCC work in international relations and public policy concerns.[26] Chappell's narrative has little use for the theology of brotherhood and inclusivity advanced by the FCC, which in fact was a profound and capacious source from which leaders like King, Benjamin Mays, and others could draw. This theological tradition and the networks through which it was propagated, particularly when filtered through the experiences of Blacks like Haynes, should be emphasized more than they have been if we are to get a fuller conception of the diverse theological and intellectual antecedents to the Black freedom struggle.[27]

When Benjamin Mays gave his stirring address before the World Council of Churches in Evanston, Illinois, in 1954, he articulated many of the same basic arguments that the FCC's leaders had been making since the 1920s. Mays's talk, entitled "The Church Amidst Ethnic and Racial Tensions," contained five points: 1) That the Old Testament drew distinctions along religious and not racial lines. 2) That in the New Testament separateness was based on religion and culture, not on race or ethnicity. 3) That slavery, imperialism, and colonization were implicated in the emergence of modern notions of race and concepts of whiteness and racial superiority. Thus, racism was an aberration in the church's history and a modern heresy. 4) That modern science indicated that there was no such thing as an inherently inferior or superior race, and modern anthropology demonstrated that human populations did not differ in their capacities for intellectual and emotional development. 5) That segregation had pernicious social and personal effects in that it hurt the pride of the person discriminated against and scarred the souls of the segregator, among other things.[28] There is no doubt that Mays' contemporary white southern critics questioned the validity of his claims or argued against his reading of Scripture, but in this talk we find a basic resonance between his ideas and the FCC's theology of brotherhood, which had challenged a theology of segregation for several decades. Mays was working within a broader trajectory of interracialism and Social Gospel thought, of which the FCC was one of the most prominent exemplars.[29]

Mays, as mentor to Martin Luther King, Jr., and as a prominent Black clergyman who challenged segregation, represented a strand of Black leadership that had worked within the upper echelons of white religious organizations. Nothing about his strong emphasis on education and his willingness to work alongside whites indicates that he should be placed within an "irrational" religious tradition that Chappell deems so important to the success of the Civil Rights movement and its challenge to segregation. A much more important development in Mays's life is his training in white liberal theological institutions in the North and his earlier work in the FCC. These experiences, and his indebtedness to this ecumenical strand of Christian thought, are illuminating in any narrative that purports to trace the intellectual antecedents of the Black freedom struggle.[30]

The FCC's actions were not in the same mold as the grassroots activism of the Civil Rights movement. My primary aim is to treat the FCC in its particular evolving historical context by arguing that its theology of brotherhood was a hard-fought achievement amidst dominant racist discourses and not an intrinsic part of the Christian tradition, as an ahistorical approach assumes. This is especially so in the American context, with its history of slavery and a dominant theology of segregation during the Jim Crow South era. This strand of Protestant Christianity is currently under scholarly reassessment regarding its long-term influence and effects in US cultural and political life. This book extends this reexamination to race. Although I examine, among other things, the way the FCC's Department of Race Relations sought to influence public policy, I keep in mind Sugrue's instructive point: "Social movements have an impact on public policy. Public policies and national politics shape and constrain the options available to activists. . . . Most protestors did not draft civil rights laws, propose legislation, or enact regulations.

But they raised issues of racial exclusion in public forums, through demonstrations, pamphlets and newspaper articles. . . . Their victories were seldom complete or wholly satisfying. . . . Advocates of racial equality—and their opponents—were very much products of their times, of a history not always of their own making."[31] This description is an apt way to narrate the significance of the FCC's racial projects, and I try to attend to their victories and their defeats in my general narrative.

The FCC had many limitations in imagining and producing substantive and lasting social change, but its Department of Race Relations laid a foundation of biblical and theological argumentation about race that was quite similar to that later articulated by leading Black and white religious figures in the Civil Rights movement. Clearly, the experiences of each of these individuals and the actual practice of their religious beliefs differed depending on local context and particular historical moment. I argue that it is worth examining the theology articulated by the FCC and its racial work (in the North and South) to substantiate this claim. Examining the FCC's race work is important precisely because it reveals something about the internal work of the churches and how they tried to address the problem of race before the emergence of the Black freedom struggle. No project of this kind, however, can be generalized to the work of most Protestant churches, but it does reveal the intersection of theology and practice for a specific ecumenical strand of Christianity.

I seek to navigate between the public and the intimate. On the one hand, I look at narratives that focus on the public dimensions of activists: that is, their attempt to influence Congress to pass national legislation, to get a hearing with the President, or to bring public attention to some egregious manifestation of racial injustice (such as lynching). On the other hand, following historian Tobin Shearer in his book, *Daily Demonstrators: The Civil Rights Movement in Mennonite Homes and Sanctuaries* (2010), I look at the arguments for social change that emerge in more intimate spaces, such as churches and homes—and how these impact narratives with more public dimensions. The FCC was a somewhat unusual example to study because it was not a church and yet it tended to work through and among churches. It was not a political faction or a grassroots movement. Some of the Department's meetings were held in homes, and all of them opened with prayer (and sometimes worship, if the meetings took place in larger settings). The FCC constantly wrestled with the question of influence: should public witness to its vision of Christian unity and justice be its principal task (primarily through educating and speaking out to the churches), or should sustaining projects with concrete and measurable goals be its chief duty? These tasks were never easily separable in practice. Nonetheless, the ecumenical vision of the FCC and its theological self-identity as a witness to Christian unity must be taken into account when thinking about its role in a broader narrative on attempts at racial justice and social change.

The first chapter begins with a description of the emergence of the Department of Race Relations. It places special emphasis on the FCC's forceful articulation of a theology of brotherhood. This capacious vision of the human family and this more inclusive notion of the nation was a minority view when first set forth in the 1920s and was foundational to the FCC's race work. The first chapter also develops in extensive detail a point already mentioned: that the FCC's racial and social work indicated a vibrant Social Gospel tradition that persisted beyond and despite the disillusionment and ravages of the First World War.[32]

In the second chapter, I look at the evolution of the Department's anti-lynching campaign, highlighting its commitment during the interwar years to facing and opposing the most brutal aspects of racial oppression. I critically assess the FCC's efforts to educate the public about the nature, number, and atrocity of lynchings, and I examine how its educational attempts at moral suasion and swaying churches encountered serious limitations when it sought to deal with lynchings in their specific and local contexts. Even so, the FCC discovered that trying to get Congress to make lynching a federal crime was also a difficult task and that the political process offered no easy solution to this instrument of terror against Black Americans. By highlighting the work of the FCC, I hope that future general narratives of the anti-lynching campaign will include the FCC alongside the National Association of Colored People (NAACP), the Commission on Interracial Cooperation (CIC), and the Association of Southern Women for the Prevention of Lynching (ASWPL), the major organizations that sought to end lynching.

Chapter three examines the various techniques and practices that the Department implemented to effecting personal and church transformation. Annual Race Relations Sundays, which began in 1923, and interracial clinics or workshops, which were founded in 1943, are the two major "tools" that I explore as a way of assessing how the FCC envisioned the problem of race and sought to undermine racial prejudice in individuals (and within churches).

Chapter four explores theological debates about the role of the church in the world and examines the interracial workshops as concrete instruments to address racial division and oppression in the postwar period.

Chapter five looks at the internal dynamics of interracialism within the FCC. It also takes a long view of the structural constraints that the FCC faced in its project of racial and social reform. I look at the internal problems of the FCC, especially its relationship with local churches and its constant budgetary constraints. The upshot is that the FCC fared reasonably well in executing its projects in light of internal and external constraints, and was rather progressive and ahead of its time in many of its public stances on racial issues, especially its rejection of segregation in 1946, nearly a decade before the *Brown* decision of 1954. While not offering an apology for the FCC, my work balances discussion of the FCC's own constraints over against the massive racial oppression and obstacles it faced (like all organizations that fought racism). Attention to both must be paid if we are to get the fullest picture of the FCC's influence and legacy.

The Department of Race Relations began with a grand and ambitious goal of demonstrating the sufficiency of Christianity to solve the race problem in America. It quickly realized that only concrete and hard-fought efforts would come near to achieving this lofty goal in any meaningful sense. These actions included fighting against the shameful practice of lynching; working with local Black farmers in the South to rectify obvious cases of abuse and economic disparity; chipping away at segregation and finally frontally assaulting it; chastising and urging churches to address racial division and bigotry within their ranks; and bringing Christians together to foster interracial cooperation and appreciation for the gifts and talents that various groups brought to their communities and to the nation. It is not clear what "demonstration" meant for the FCC. Was it a process of witnessing by words—and indeed, there were many spoken and written by the FCC? Was this a witness by works to the ideals of Christianity? Was it, as one of its memos stated, a willingness of Christians to suffer and experience hardship in their fight against injustice and racial prejudice? How and by whom would this demonstration be judged? Was it to be concluded in time at some particular moment? On what was this "sufficiency" of Christianity based—on certain kinds of actions exhibited by Christians? And how precisely was this sufficiency defined? Perhaps the FCC's efforts to end racial oppression necessarily seem modest in view of these grand goals. Nevertheless, its racial work did demonstrate that Christians united by a rich theological vision of "faith in the possibility of a new social order," and working together, could ameliorate gross manifestations of injustice and bear witness to a more inclusive vision of humanity and the church.[33]

1

A Protestant Theology of Brotherhood

During its first meeting on July 12, 1921, held in Washington, DC at 10 o'clock in the morning, the Commission on Negro Churches and Race Relations of the FCC spelled out its analysis of the problem of race in America. Robert Speer, the president of the FCC, called the meeting to order and spoke briefly about the requests of Southern representatives, Black and white, to form a commission that specifically addressed racial issues. Speer stated that the problem of the "relations of the races" was the most difficult one facing humanity and presented "the most searching test" of Christian ideals and principles. He forcefully proclaimed that all gathered shared fundamental and common beliefs: God as the common father of all; humanity as an organ of the divine; and that all are bound together "in one bundle of life." Given these shared premises, Speer noted, they were "committed to the method of cooperation and must, therefore, find ways of living together in mutual helpfulness, service and goodwill." Especially in America, he asserted, where the race problem existed in its most acute form, Christians had the "greatest opportunity in the world to make a constructive contribution to its solution." For Speer, the "mere existence" of the commission would be testimony "to the fact that in Christianity there is a real solution for our inter-racial problem and that the churches are going to deal courageously with their responsibility of seeing that the Christian solution is achieved." He expressed grave concern about the consequences if the church should fail to address racial conflict, noting that home and international missionary work would suffer as a result. If, however, the church could deal successfully with its "racial problem in an effective way at home," Speer concluded, the results would be "an undreamed of access of power to the Church on the foreign field."[1]

It was fitting that Speer would end his talk about how race relations in the United States figured in the churches' missionary work. After having served as a traveling secretary for the Student Volunteer Movement, which was formed in the late nineteenth century to recruit students for foreign missions, Speer became a secretary of the Presbyterian Board of Foreign Missions. As Robert Handy notes, he was among a leading cadre of Protestant laymen who encouraged the churches to emphasize "missionary work as the way to save souls in distant places and to advance civilization across the globe."[2] Handy and William R. Hutchison argue that Speer was especially important in his influence on churches because of his ability to bridge the gap between conservative and liberal Protestants before the lines between these groups hardened in the latter part of the 1920s.[3] Speer's comments about the FCC's commission on race and Black churches reflected several persisting concerns of its racial work, which commenced in earnest in the 1920s. First, there was an acute sense that Christianity's reputation was at stake to the extent that it failed to solve the race problem in the US. Second, there was a heightened fear that missionary work would suffer immensely if Christian civilization in the US could not eliminate the worst abuses of racial violence and discrimination, such as lynching and race riots. Third, the council's theology of brotherhood and inclusivity appeared to be hollow words in view of the churches' relative silence on the segregation of Blacks in the South and racial discrimination and restrictions in the North. After many speeches, the commission offered a number of theological and concrete proposals. First on the list was the following proposition: "to assert the sufficiency of Christianity as the solution of race relations in America and the duty of the Churches and all other organizations to give the most careful attention to the question."[4]

The FCC had been formed as a public body in 1908, in the midst of spirited debates about restraining the power of corporations in public life and giving laborers their fair share in the industrial world. For the next decade and a half, fairness in labor relations was a central concern of the FCC, which adopted an already existing Labor Sunday upon its formation and served as an arbiter in labor disputes during the First World War. The FCC was also heir to the ecumenical impulse that sought to bring greater unity to the churches as the visible body of Christ and to promote public witness of the churches beyond their local situation in the United States.[5] There was an awareness of, in part through missionary activity, the interrelatedness of different cultures and peoples in the broader church. This international dimension of the churches helped some within the FCC to be more conscious of how the problem of racial division and oppression in America could become or was already a blot on their witness of the Christian gospel.

The FCC was also part of and a development within the broader transformation of a segment of Christianity in the United States in the early twentieth century. Rather than seeing the world as a lost place from which to rescue the elect, FCC leaders increasingly conceived of changing the world into a human brotherhood. This Social Gospel strand of Christianity increasingly emphasized social structures and placed less emphasis on doctrinal creeds.[6] Yet there was no straightforward or obvious reason why the FCC would become more involved in racial issues than other, more conservative Christian organizations did.

So why did the FCC become actively involved in trying to deal with the nation's racial problems in the 1920s? Was it primarily or exclusively because of massive migration of Blacks from the South to the urban North and Midwest? Was the FCC similar to the Urban League and other organizations that sought to address what they saw as the problems of temporary adjustment that a rural folk must endure in moving to such a different environment? The FCC, unlike the Urban League, did not look at the problem of race primarily in terms of adjustment to an urban context, though Black migration was a crucial catalyst for its concentrated attention to the problem of race. The FCC's international work as an interdenominational Protestant organization and its more capacious theology, rooted in the Social Gospel emphasis on social solidarity and human interrelatedness, are two major factors in its turn to race in the 1920s and its subsequent sustained commitment to racial justice. Its openness and contributions to the social sciences that affirmed the unity of humanity and rejected invidious distinctions between or hierarchical ordering of races were both an expression of its dissent from dominant racial ideologies of the time and a reflection of its broader theology of brotherhood. Its emphasis on social structures made race difficult to avoid, but its reconceiving of the world as a potential human brotherhood was surely a catalyst in the struggle to defeat racial oppression.

Race in American Religious Life

By the turn of the twentieth century and well beyond the 1920s, even in the North, a consensus on race and race relations had emerged in American intellectual circles. The *Plessy v. Ferguson* majority ruling (1896) expressed the legal version of this consensus: "Legislation is powerless to eradicate racial instincts or to abolish distinctions based on physical differences, and the attempt to do so can only result in accentuating the difficulties of the present situation. . . . If one race be inferior to the other socially, the Constitution of the United States cannot put them upon the same plane."[7] The US Supreme Court affirmed racial distinctions and enshrined in law scientific racism. Scientific racism was shared by northern and southern theorists, with its popular and religious forms varying in both regions. It dominated American social thought and was widespread in universities. The consensus on racial thought at the turn of the century might be summarized in the following propositions: that Blacks were physically, intellectually, and temperamentally different from whites; that Blacks were inferior to whites in at least certain fundamental areas: intelligence, initiative, and self-governance; these differences were either permanent or subject to change only by a slow evolutionary process; miscegenation or intermarriage should be strongly discouraged or proscribed by law; racial prejudice was natural and an inevitable white response to Blacks when they were free or aspiring to equal status; and a fully biracial or integrated society was therefore either completely impossible or could only be achieved in a remote and almost inconceivable future. Thus, the destiny of Blacks in the US was to be either indefinite subordination or elimination (through colonization or deportation).[8]

These were not merely abstract notions about racial difference. From the 1890s to the 1950s, the American Jim Crow South was an overtly racist regime. George Frederickson defines an overtly racist regime as a state that codified and enforced racist principles by laws and that made them a central concern of public policy. In this historical context, racism was more than theorizing about human differences or thinking badly of a group over which one had no control. As is well known to historians of the South, racism entailed a notion of difference and power, a mindset that regarded "them" (Blacks) as different from "us" (whites) in ways that are permanent. This sense of difference provided the motive for using whites' power advantage to treat African Americans in a number of unjust and differential ways.[9]

Overtly racist regimes such as that of the South, while they espouse an official ideology that is explicitly racist, must insistently claim that the differences between the dominant group and the one being dominated are permanent and unbridgeable. This sense of racial difference was expressed clearly in laws forbidding interracial marriage. The ideal was "race purity." Social segregation was thus mandated by law, with its object being the barring of all forms of contact that might imply equality. As leaders of the FCC came to realize, in overtly racist regimes, social segregation, though it may exist on different levels, is not merely left to custom or private acts of discrimination that are tolerated by the state. The state places its force in the forms of laws and regulations to uphold and maintain this form of segregation. To the extent that the regime claims a formal democratic polity, it excludes outgroup members from holding public office or having the right to vote. Invariably, access to resources and economic opportunities is severely limited, thus keeping the stigmatized group in poverty.[10]

This contemporary definition of racism is illuminating in that it is remarkably similar to some of the prescient ways that the FCC came to understand race relations in the nation. Its interpretation of racial oppression had a profound impact on some of its proposals to undermine it. While the FCC's concrete efforts were crucial to its project to address race in the US (especially its anti-lynching campaign and its eventual support of a legal dismantling of segregation in the South), its theology of brotherhood rooted in a Social Gospel Protestant ethos was, itself, significant. There is still debate among historians about the extent of commitment to racial reform within Social Gospel Protestantism. Recent scholarship points to the American Missionary Association's involvement with Blacks in the South and notes the antebellum roots of northern missionary efforts among Blacks in the South. Ralph Luker suggests that racial issues were a major concern for Social Gospel leaders, though he identifies almost any Protestant reform of the time with the Social Gospel, depriving it of explanatory specificity. I remain unconvinced that racial issues were central to the reforms of Social Gospel leaders such as Washington Gladden and Walter Rauschenbusch. Both were much more concerned about the problems of labor and industrialization; African Americans and race were not central to their thinking. Edward Blum's *Reforging the White Republic* argues that Protestant Christianity in the North helped to forge a new sense of white American nationalism that solidified by the end of the nineteenth century and "sanctified" the segregation of Blacks in the South. Northern Protestants, according to Blum, played a crucial role in reuniting the North and South and in justifying the segregation of Blacks in the South (Blum does not specifically address the arguments of Luker and White, and his narrative ends in 1898).[11] Prior to the First World War and the Great Migration of Blacks to the urban Northeast and Midwest, there is little evidence that racial reform was central to northern Protestants, whether or not they were a part of the Social Gospel reform impulse.

In general, the differences between southern and northern white churches can be summarized in the following manner: though in 1900 most northern churches were still segregated (like their southern counterparts), some of them had an anti-slavery past. Northerners were so consumed by the problems of urbanization, industrialization, and massive immigration in the first decade of the century that they could for the most part conveniently ignore Blacks in their midst. Among northern religious leaders, there was a deep fear of emotionalism, southern revivalism, and Black folk religious practices. Although these leaders tended to be uninterested in reiterating a biblical defense of segregation, as was dominant in the South, there was a constant struggle with custom and local practice, which favored segregation. What emerged at the turn of the century was an internal struggle of separation within denominations, in which all-Black congregations within a larger denominational body formed in part because of residential segregation and congregational preferences. But in both the South and North, there were a variety of views even within this racially divided context.

There was a range of positions advocated by what Ralph Luker calls "theologians of race relations" in the early twentieth century. What I focus on in this book are those who emerged from or were in basic sympathy with what Luker calls "radical transformationists."[12] The radical transformationists held that Black Americans should enter the mainstream, but would also make their own contribution, thus transforming what it meant to be an American. This was a small minority of American Christians, and it was out of this context of Social Gospel Christian advocates or evangelical neoabolitionists that the FCC emerged.[13] This theology of brotherhood had several components that made it a somewhat radical and certainly a dissenting minority view in its historical context. It argued for the unity of humanity, and though its advocates may have differed about specific proposals, they tended to reject the dominant scientific racism in the United States and eventually moved toward a frontal assault on segregation. They often interpreted lynching and other forms of violence against Blacks as the most manifest exhibition of a social system that oppressed and denigrated Black Americans. They highlighted and uplifted the contributions that Blacks made to American culture and sought ways to bring about positive social interactions between Blacks and whites. A few imagined a multiracial democracy where Blacks, whites, and other ethnic groups created and forged a new nation where racial inequality was not the basis of its organization and polity.

Articulating a theology of brotherhood that had as its central claims the unity of humanity, a critique of hierarchal ranking of races, and the church as a democracy of sinners in need of grace, was as major a challenge to the dominant southern theology of separation as it was to the scientific racism that pervaded American intellectual life. From the post-Civil War period well into the 1950s, southern politicians, judges, and religious leaders appealed to the Bible as the basis for laws against interracial marriage, arguing that God created separate and hierarchical races with whites as the dominant race. This theology of separate races served as a key rationale for anti-miscegenation statutes in the Jim Crow South, and its racial identity laws.[14] The FCC's views of race thus placed it in direct opposition to dominant theological and scientific conceptions of race. Its theology of brotherhood was a fundamental critique of the ideological foundations of scientific and religious racism. Yet the FCC also had to find a way to deal with external critiques of itself by churches, and to address the racism exhibited and sustained by practicing Christians among members of its own constituency. The very efficacy of Christian faith to confront and ameliorate racial division became a pressing issue, especially in the context of international missionary work.

The Meaning of Brotherhood

In 1924, Arthur Holt and F. Ernest Johnson succinctly stated the central meaning of Christian brotherhood: "It is our view that the chief purpose which Jesus came to further was the building of a spiritual brotherhood inclusive of all mankind, and that the central thing, therefore, in Christianity is the ideal and the practice of fellowship."[15] Holt was the secretary of the Social Service Commission of the Congregational Education Society in Boston, and worked closely with the FCC's Social Service

Commission in planning industrial conferences.[16] Johnson (discussed further in Chapter 4) was secretary of the FCC's Research and Education Department. Both men were prominent figures within the upper echelons of ecumenical Protestantism, articulating its central ideals for industrial life in the mid-1920s. Yet brotherhood as a more capacious and inclusive understanding of human connection has its roots in the nineteenth century. One of the common slogans of liberal Christianity in the mid-nineteenth century was "the fatherhood of God and the brotherhood of man." Charles Howard Hopkins noted in his seminal work that this formulation was "of fundamental importance to the social gospel."[17] As he did with so many other theological developments in the late nineteenth century, Washington Gladden wrote down his thoughts on what he called the "Ruling Ideas of the Present Age" in 1895. Gladden offered his view of the implications of a right understanding of God's fatherhood and human brotherhood: "The coming of the kingdom of heaven will be signalized and hastened by the prevalence of clearer ideas respecting the brotherhood of man. When the doctrine of Divine Fatherhood is rightly understood, the conceptions of men respecting their relations to one another must needs be clarified."[18] Gladden believed that God's fatherhood as personal father of all humanity meant a more authentic relationship between Christians and non-Christians, and thus a rejection of a conception of fatherhood as limited only to the "regenerate." He drew out a number of ideal implications from this theological conviction. Gladden argued that it led to democracy because it put all humans on an equal playing field as children of God. It condemned all forms of oppression and belittling of fellow human beings because it maintained their equal status as the offspring of God. Gladden also noted that some "measure of social fellowship must also follow" from this doctrine that insisted that all are equal in the eyes of God and therefore are entitled to respect and reverence, not merely those who share similar tastes and aptitudes.[19]

Although the emphasis on brotherhood and human connection is pronounced in the writings of Social Gospel leaders, it is just as striking that their writings evince worry and a sense of almost impotence about their failure to connect with and reach the working classes. Inability to surmount class differences was the central failure in their assessments of the practical implications of this rediscovery of Christian brotherhood. Gladden identified wage workers (the industrial masses) and the poor as a major challenge for modern social Christianity, despite its claims about social solidarity, brotherhood, and concern for economic life. He wrote: "Certain it is that Christianity can never cure the social ills under which we are suffering while so large a class remains practically untouched by its healing influences."[20] Gladden acknowledged that wage workers had justifiable reasons to feel alienated from the churches. Their bosses attended such ornate churches and yet treated them as mere laboring machines with whom they had only a "cash nexus." Workers wanted justice, fair wages, better working conditions, respect, and churches where they were not reminded of the impassable wealth divide between them and their bosses, who often funded these churches. Gladden reminded his readers that employers should see their workers as their neighbors (taking his cue from the parable of the Good Samaritan in Luke 10:25–37) and reject an antagonistic (as opposed to a cooperative) view of labor and management.[21]

In several of his writings, Gladden moved beyond reflections on labor and the working class to argue that this "new evangelism" of the Social Gospel had as one of its principal objectives the redemption of society—and that included reconciliation between the races. In short, Gladden believed that a theology of brotherhood would lead to a democratization of the church, respect for the dignity of the working classes and attempts to reincorporate them into the church, and earnest endeavors to bring the races together and create a society of mutual respect and sharing of power. Most of Gladden's writings about race and African Americans were rather vague and general compared to his discussions of labor and the industrial working classes, but as a leading exponent of Social Gospel ideas and a popularizer of liberal Protestant theology up until his death in 1918, he served as an important transitional figure. Gladden was the chief interpreter of Christian brotherhood and its implications for social reform.[22] The FCC's Department of Race Relations would take up more pragmatically the implications of a theology of brotherhood and develop its specific ramifications for African Americans and race relations more generally in the US, but Gladden and others were key players in promulgating this theology of brotherhood before the FCC's formation in 1908.[23]

A theology of brotherhood was even more central to the religious and social thought of African American religious leaders who regularly asserted that American white Christianity was deficient on this score. Reverdy Ransom and Francis Grimké, though in two different denominations and theological traditions, converged in their affirmation of brotherhood as foundational to Christianity. Ransom was a leading AME minister and had important connections with key white proponents of Social Christianity. He delivered a scathing critique of racism in white Christian churches in an address to the National Reform Convention at Park Street Congregational Church in Boston, Massachusetts, in 1905. Ransom started his talk with a forceful claim about the meaning of Acts 17:26: "God hath made of one blood all nations of men for to dwell on all the face of the earth." The point of this passage and the beginnings of the Pentecostal origins of the church for Ransom was that "Jesus Christ founded Christianity in the midst of the most bitter and intense antagonisms of race and class."[24] He asserted that Jesus transcended ("ignored") these racial divisions and, while he conceded that "the Jewish religion and the entire social and political structure of Hebrew civilization rested upon the idea of race," he said that Judaism's ultimate goal was to establish the idea of one God. Ultimately, it was upon this foundation that Jesus built the "superstructure of 'the Fatherhood of God,' and its corollary, 'the Brotherhood of man.'" All of these previous historical developments led to the "crowning object" for which Jesus aimed, the breaking down of the walls between humans and reconciliation of Jew and Gentile into one body through Jesus.[25]

Ransom was adamant that the problem of race was "the most serious problem in our country today." He directly measured and assessed

Christian ethics by its ability to mitigate and ultimately confront the problem of race head on. Ransom emphatically stated: "American Christianity will un-Christ itself if it refuses to strive on, until this Race Problem is not only settled, but settled right." In tallying the various ways in which Blacks were subjugated and humiliated in American society, he raised serious doubts about its professed Christianity. Ransom undoubtedly shocked his audience when he angrily stated: "If this be the spirit of Jesus, then give us Mohammed or any other redeemer."[26] He and other African American Social Gospel leaders regarded brotherhood or human connection that transcended race as foundational to Christian faith. It was their test of its efficacy and divinity. For some like Ransom, Christianity's potential ability to make racial differences into positive human connections and a fuller humanity was precisely what could make the American experiment unique and distinctive. As Ransom noted: "As God is above man, so man is above race. There is nothing to fear by demolishing every wall, religious political, industrial, social that separates man from his brotherman. God has given us a splendid heritage here upon these shores; he has made us the pioneers of liberty for all mankind. He has placed the Negro and white man here for centuries, to grow side by side . . . thus will these two peoples one at last become the school masters of all the world, teaching by examples the brotherhood of man."[27] These were indeed grand and heady claims, born of faith in Jesus and a hopeful vision of America that rested uneasily and in tension with Ransom's enumeration and elaboration of the brutal and harsh racial oppression that African Americans endured at the turn of the twentieth century. Yet Ransom maintained an eschatological optimism about the power of Christian faith to realize this vision of brotherhood. He concluded: "If the new Jerusalem tarries in its descent to earth, coming down from God out of heaven, then we, not like some foolish tower-builders upon the plains of Shinar, but taught from heaven in a better way, shall build upon the teachings of Jesus, with the doctrine of human brotherhood as taught by Him, until fraternity realized, shall raise us to the skies."[28] The reference to the "plains of

Shinar" was an allusion to Genesis 11, a story of human hubris attempting to reach the heavens and attain unity of speech and purpose amidst human differences. In the story, God frustrates the plans of humans. As a Christian, Ransom apparently read this Hebrew text as a thwarted and premature endeavor at human brotherhood that was supplanted by "a better way" through the teachings and ethics of Jesus. Through Jesus and the growth of the Christian state, now this was a possible achievement, a divine moment.

Another important African American leader who articulated this theology of brotherhood was Francis J. Grimké, the pastor of Fifteenth Street Presbyterian Church in Washington, DC, at the turn of the century.[29] In his 1910 address "Christianity and Race Prejudice," Grimké developed one of his fullest explanations of the relationship between Christianity and the problem of "race prejudice." He laid out several principles of Christianity that he felt were foundational to Jesus's mission and identity, and directly antithetical to racial discrimination in the Christian life and the corporate witness of Christian churches. These principles were the following pillars of his thought: the fatherhood of God, the brotherhood of man, the Golden Rule, the second and great commandment ("thou shalt love thy neighbor as thyself"), Paul's admonition that we follow the things that make for peace and that edify each other, and that all Christians are one in Jesus Christ, which means that together believers constitute one family.

Grimké wrote at length and with eagerness about the fatherhood of God and the brotherhood of man, no doubt because he saw them as providing an alternative or opposing theology to a theology of racial separation. He ascribed signal importance to these two concepts. Grimké wrote:

> And so we are all sons and daughters of one common father. The Fatherhood of God. This is a great thought! How it lifts the whole plane of humanity! What dignity it gives to every human being, however humble, however lowly! It doesn't make any difference how poor, how ignorant we

> may be, to what race we belong, whether we are in bondage or not, the relationship exists all the same. Poverty, ignorance, race affiliation can not change, in the least; the fact that God is our Father. All men are children of God, Jesus taught. . . . If God is our Father then, of course, we are all brothers. Jesus taught the brotherhood of man. Literally this is true—men are brothers—the human race is one.[30]

In studying the ministries and examples of Grimké and other African American leaders, it is clear that race was crucial to a Christian Social Gospel in modern America, and that the ethics and efficacy of Christianity in realizing brotherhood were their consistent tests of its relevance and divine truthfulness.

Demonstrating the Sufficiency of Christianity to Solve the Race Problem

The FCC was particularly concerned about the legitimacy of Christian faith in the modern world and the efficacy of Christianity to solve racial problems, given both the long and the immediate history in the US of Black and white criticisms of Christianity's record on race. Edward Blum has demonstrated in several of his works how leading African Americans, from the Civil War to the early twentieth century, challenged the claim that the US was a Christian nation—not so much on legal grounds and contested meanings of the Constitution, but on moral grounds.[31] Ida B. Wells and others asked: How could a Christian nation allow its citizens to burn alive fellow human beings? W. E. B. Du Bois often posed the following question in his many writings: Would not Jesus, the lowly Jew from Nazareth, side with oppressed and lynched African Americans? Du Bois constantly excoriated Christian churches for their hypocrisy and poor record on race relations.[32] These kinds of criticisms grew more vocal over time and were especially directed at leading evangelists and public figures who supported segregation or who ignored the problem of race. In 1903, Kelly Miller, a professor of sociology at

Howard University, gave a talk on "The Negro Church" at Atlanta with a seemingly optimistic title, "Religion as the Solvent of the Race Problem." Yet in the actual speech Miller expressed grave doubts about the ability of Christianity to wean Anglo-Saxons (using the racial terminology of his day) from race prejudice, and stated that, for most white Americans, ethnic ties were much stronger than spiritual kinship with those of a different race or ethnicity who shared the Christian faith. Miller wondered if God was using Black Americans to help whites to understand that "race idolatry" was a serious sin and that they needed to practice the "concrete brotherhood of man."[33] This was a reversal of Christian witness for Miller, in which Blacks, who in significant numbers had accepted Christianity under a regime of slavery, would now teach whites its true meaning of brotherly love.

Black leaders were particularly angry at public figures who claimed that their faith animated their public service and yet who supported segregation and had little concern for the plight of African Americans. Perhaps no Black leader was as consistent over the years in his assault against racism in American Christianity as Francis Grimké. Grimké preached from his noted church in the nation's capital, a prominent Black church with doctors, lawyers, and teachers in attendance.[34] In 1922, in a sermon entitled, "What is the Trouble with the Christianity of Today? There is Something Wrong about it. What is it?" Grimké accused the Christianity of his day of gross hypocrisy in its refusal to practice its professed belief in the fatherhood of God and the brotherhood of man. He noted, "Everywhere [the church] is setting up barriers against men on account of race and color." Grimké condemned American white Christians for practicing a religion "that lays greater emphasis upon the color of a man's skin than upon his Christian character."[35]

Grimké focused on two public figures, both Presbyterians, to demonstrate examples of Christian racism: former President Woodrow Wilson and William Jennings Bryan, who, though formerly secretary of state and three-time candidate for the presidency, was then promoting real estate in Florida and deepening his involvement in the anti-evolution crusade. Of Wilson, Grimké wrote, "I have very little faith in the Christianity of Mr. Woodrow Wilson." He asked, "How can our civilization become permeated with the spirit of Christ, when professing Christians, like Mr. Woodrow Wilson and Mr. William Jennings Bryan, outstanding figures, in the church, go on preaching and practicing the kind of Christianity which they represent?" Grimké and other Blacks still felt anger and a sense of betrayal over Wilson's cabinet, which had formally backed federal segregation.

Bryan had referred to an anti-lynching bill in the House of Representatives as a grave mistake and basically defended Jim Crow. Jim Crow segregation never really bothered Bryan.[36] In light of these kinds of approaches to faith and practice, Grimké presented the color-line as one of the greatest obstacles to the spread of Christianity. He proclaimed: "A cowardly, time-serving, unbrotherly, stiff-necked uncircumcised, color-prejudiced Christianity can never save this world, can never bring it to Christ—a world two-thirds of the inhabitants of which are not white but colored." For Grimké, Christianity's record on race stood as its acid test.

This criticism of the efficacy and ethics of Christianity in America was not simply directed at the hypocrisy of white Christians. Some turned their anger at Blacks' acceptance of the Christian faith. Though both Black and white leaders were involved in this critique, one example of a prominent white critic demonstrates the point. In 1925, Clarence Darrow, notably described as a famous atheist and criminal lawyer by a respected Black news weekly, gave a widely touted speech for the NAACP at Salem Methodist Episcopal church in Harlem. Four thousand people were present, and others had to be turned away because of overcrowding. Darrow had gained the appellation of "friend of the Negro" because of his work on behalf of the NAACP. He began his address, which lasted an hour and a half, with these provocative words: "I don't know whether the Almighty delivered Daniel from the lion's den or not, but if he did, it's about time he was working another such miracle in behalf of Negroes in this country." A number of prominent Black ministers were shocked by Darrow's comments. In an unexpected transition in his speech, Darrow criticized Blacks for their religion. "You're too blooming pious," he counseled Blacks. "It's time you realize that if the Almighty was going to do anything for you he would have done it long ago. I have a suspicion that He is a Nordic anyway. The more Negroes find they can't depend on Daniel and the Lord but get busy themselves, the further they will get along."[37] On the following day, Darrow delivered a speech in a large Unitarian church, and though he praised those gathered for their progressive stance on social issues, he asked if any in a crowd of almost two thousand personally knew any Blacks. Two or three sheepishly raised their hands.

These kinds of criticisms were also uttered by a number of secular Black leaders. They agreed that Christianity prohibited Blacks from advancing and that it was a white man's religion in any case. I have focused especially on Darrow and Bryan because we often associate them with the Scopes Trial and the fundamentalist-modernist controversy, emphasizing such issues as evolution, historical criticism of the Bible, and skepticism about the claims of Christianity. My analysis, however, suggests we need to broaden our angle about the ways in which the practice of Christianity in America was challenged not primarily on the basis of intellectual concerns, but more often in the realm of ethics and efficacy.[38]

In this intellectual context, the FCC began its work on race relations. Its concerted involvement in race relations was prompted, however, by the situation created by the First World War. The War-Time Commission of the FCC asked the Committee on Negro Churches to study the needs of Black troops. This special wartime committee helped to pave the way for a permanent Commission on Negro Churches and Race Relations.[39] More generally, the movement of Blacks from the South to the Midwest and North gave rise to grave fears among many northern whites. Race riots across the country in 1919 and the nationalization of what had previously been regarded as a southern Negro problem led a number of northern white church leaders to begin addressing the concrete conditions that Blacks faced.[40] On the morning of June 1, 1921, about six weeks before Speer convened the first meeting of what was to become the Department of Race Relations, white rioters burned and looted Greenwood, the Black section of Tulsa, Oklahoma, one of the most devastating race riots in American history.[41] Deep worries about continuing racial violence contributed to the Department's formation and Black leaders gathered were especially vocal in their calls for protection against lynching.

While there was a time lag between the founding of the FCC in 1908 and 1921, when its Commission on Negro Churches and Race Relations was organized, its formation indicates that there was a growing consciousness about racism in the churches in the aftermath of the First World War. Though fears and anxieties about an increasing Black presence in urban areas were catalysts, some leaders in the FCC began to experience the problem of race as "our problem" and not simply as a southern or Negro problem. Speer's public address, mentioned earlier, provides some sense of the idealism and heightened expectancy that many of these early leaders expressed.

The Contours and Contents of a Theology of Brotherhood

From its very first meeting, the FCC's Commission on Negro Churches and Race Relations (hereafter mostly referred to as its Department of Race Relations) held that the churches had a moral and spiritual duty in "bringing about inter-racial brotherhood." As noted earlier, Robert Speer's opening address urged church members to think of themselves as "all bound together in one bundle of life." The very language used indicates a change in perspective on the problem of race and a fundamental reorientation in theologies of race. No longer was this called the Negro Problem, but "race relations" now implied a dynamism about race that sent no distinct overtone about superiority or inferiority of races. The "fundamental theory of race relations" that Speer articulated was an extension of Social Gospel emphases that had gained ascendancy among a number of leading Protestant bodies, but that had their origin in the late nineteenth century, as noted above. These themes included: "God as the common Father of all;" "humanity as an organ" of the divine; all being bound together; "the method of cooperation;" and finding ways of "living together in mutual helpfulness, service, and goodwill."[42] All of these emphases, especially the fatherhood of God, the unity of humanity, social solidarity, and cooperation, were central aspects of social Christianity since the late 1880s.[43] The FCC was an heir to these theological and social developments, and refined and extended them to the problem of race in America.

The FCC tried to realize and apply aspects of this theology of brotherhood in this first meeting, especially the themes of mutual helpfulness and cooperation. Black churches were constituent members of the FCC, notably the Colored Methodist Episcopal Church in America and the National Baptist Convention. At this gathering, Black men and women were part of the personnel and leadership team of the commission. Present were figures such as Nannie Helen Burroughs, then principal of the National Training School for Girls; Mary McLeod Bethune, Daytona Normal Institute; Kelly Miller, Howard University; and other notable names. Black leaders also took to the floor and spoke rather frankly about how the churches were failing to do their part in dealing with racial problems. Professor John R. Hawkins, financial secretary of the African Methodist Episcopal Church, opened the discussion on "What Can Churches Do as Churches to Better Race Relations," urging the churches "to get the Christian pulpit, both Negro and white, to hold up the racial question to the light of the question as to whether any existing practice or any proposed step is right." Hawkins bluntly stated that race relations had deteriorated from what they had been twenty years prior, and called for the abolition of lynching and peonage, equal facilities for travel and education, and a single moral standard for Blacks and whites. He insisted that the church should "create a new conscience on race relations."[44]

Most Black speakers dealt with concrete issues when talking about the tasks of the church, giving specificity and real-world content to a theology of brotherhood. They also sought to demonstrate that the reputation of Christianity as a missionary religion was at stake, to the extent that it failed to deal successfully with racial division in the US. Channing H. Tobias, a minister in the Colored Methodist Church, called for a single standard of citizenship, both in its privileges and responsibilities. Blacks must have justice in the courts and protection from mob violence (the terrifying violence of the lynch mob figured in almost all Black discussions of the race problem). Tobias struck a nerve that was sure to gain the attention of the missionary-oriented FCC, asserting that the church's "failure to practice its ideal of democracy in the relations of the races in our own country is preventing it from proclaiming more than a fractional message to the non-Christian world." He urged the FCC not to bring Blacks in "only as an after-thought when all plans have been made." Tobias offered to the commission several suggestions: churches should "seek through reciprocity in pulpits" to address the problems of "each race from the angle of the other," pastors must demonstrate "moral courage in the pulpit in dealing with the racial question," and the commission might use its influence to get missionary boards to send Blacks as missionaries and secure "governmental regulation" to make this possible.[45]

While many of these suggestions were directed specifically to churches, some African American speakers went beyond narrowly conceiving the problem of race in terms of what churches could do or failed to do, though clearly churches and the FCC as a representative of churches were in view, since this was a meeting convened by the FCC. George Haynes, then recording secretary pro tem and formerly director of Negro Economics at the Department of Labor, outlined four practical things for the commission to undertake: 1) through the press, pulpit, "moving picture agencies," and conversation, create propaganda to foster right attitudes and consciousness as a basis of goodwill between the races; 2) improve the conditions of Black workers and their relationships with white workers and their employers; 3) provide for Black education, especially institutions of higher learning; 4) promote conferences, meetings, and committees for personal contacts between Black and white men and women as a means of creating confidence and harmony in the relations between the races.[46] (Haynes would later implement many of these proposals after he became the lead secretary of the FCC's Department of Race Relations.) At this meeting, it was clear that Black leaders were given a voice and an unrestricted forum to air their views. They spoke openly and graphically about the problems that confronted African Americans, ranging from the violence of the lynch mob to disfranchisement. They brought concrete proposals and specific demands for justice that injected a note of realism and a call for actual improvements in social relations in the kind of conferences that often easily descended into abstractions and verbal expressions of goodwill.

Before the commission announced the specific proposals that it had adopted, it offered a theological preface. It read in its entirety:

> In organizing the Commission on Negro Churches and Race Relations at the invitation of the Federal Council of Churches of Christ in America we are animated by the conviction that the Christian religion affords the one adequate solution of the problem of races to each other. Recognizing one God as the Father of all, and conceiving of mankind as His family, we are convinced that all races are so bound together in an organized unity that only on the basis of brotherhood can satisfactory relations be secured. The Christian conception of God and man constrains us to believe wholeheartedly that the races should and can live together in mutual helpfulness and goodwill, each making its own contribution to the richness of the human family as a whole and cooperating with the others in seeking the common good.[47]

This theology of brotherhood remained at the heart of the FCC's race relations project from that moment until the FCC's incorporation into the National Council of Churches in 1950. This theological foundation undergirded its Race Relations Sundays (which began in 1923), its interracial clinics, its Brotherhood Month celebrations, its massive literature campaign, its long and unsuccessful attempt to secure a federal anti-lynching bill, its efforts to educate and assist poor Black farmers in the South, its pulpit exchanges between Black and white pastors, its promotion of Black arts and cultural achievements, and its call upon the nation and the churches to practice more just race relations. It also underpinned its formal critique of segregation that was articulated in 1946 at a special meeting of the Council in Columbus, Ohio.

The commission adopted several proposals, ranging from a general statement of the "sufficiency of Christianity as the solution of race relations in America" to specific plans to "encourage efforts for the welfare of Negro workers and the improvement of relations between employers, Negro workers and white workers." The commission committed itself to enlisting the aid of Christian churches "against mob violence" and their "support in a special program of education on the subject for a period of at least five years" (the anti-lynching campaign would eventually last for over two decades). Besides its proposed work to assist Black workers and deal with the problem of lynching, much of the commission's report highlighted its responsibility for and future commitment to distributing accurate knowledge about the facts of race relations and racial attitudes, fostering a public conscience that it hoped would secure for Blacks "equitable provision for education, health, housing, recreation and all other aspects of community welfare," and making known and supporting Christian solutions to and presentations about racial problems throughout the country.[48] The campaign against lynching, the efforts to create a public conscience on racial problems (especially through projects such as Race Relations Sunday and interracial clinics or workshops), and the FCC's massive dissemination of literature on racial problems and racial attitudes will be examined in further detail in later chapters of this work.

What is significant about this first meeting is that the FCC's theology of brotherhood eventuated in the creation of specific proposals in part as a concrete expression of Black demands, some of which were aired on the very floor of this gathering. The FCC took a two-pronged approach to the problem of race. First, it dealt with structural dimensions of racial oppression in America: economic inequality as manifested in employment, housing, health, criminal justice, and education. This also included its reflections on and commitment to address injustice in the courts and pervasive violence against African Americans. Second, the structural dimension was coupled with efforts at attitudinal change and moral suasion. Race Relations Sundays were particularly designed to bridge racial divisions within churches, bringing Blacks and whites together in peaceful settings to worship as one body and to learn more about each other. The dissemination of literature was intended to create a more accurate understanding of racial problems and to educate the public on the roots of racial prejudice. All of this was designed to change attitudes, alongside the more targeted projects to help Black farmers and campaign for a federal anti-lynching bill. Clearly, leaders in the FCC realized that distributing literature was not going to make a serious dent in racial inequality in America. The infrequency of Race Relations Sundays was hardly sufficient to affect in any substantive manner the practice of segregated Christianity in America, especially in the South. Even so, the FCC's project for racial reform, for all its structural, financial, and chronological limitations, was a remarkable and innovative program to change the basic structure of American race relations.

Christianizing the American Nation

The emergence of the FCC's race relations project occurred in a social and cultural context that has been variously and sometimes contradictorily described by historians. The 1920s has been rendered by a number of strong descriptors: roaring, tribal, and modern, among others.[49] A body of scholarship has noted the revolt against Victorian cultural hegemony, manifested in fields such as anthropology and the social sciences. Opinions about race underwent drastic changes as the disciples and students of anthropologist Franz Boas challenged standard beliefs about the inferiority of African Americans and rejected the dominant scientific racism of the time. As Stanley Corben writes, "As a result of the all but unanimous rejection of racism by scholars most involved in the study of race, the ideas of Boas and his disciples thus became the conventional wisdom of intellectuals, insinuated by them throughout American society, especially through educational institutions and the higher courts."[50] Corben dates the beginnings of this shift in thinking on race to the late 1920s.[51] There is much to be said about the significance of this transformation in theorizing about race, though its depth and influence has often been overstated. The FCC made important contributions to this intellectual shift in detaching race from culture and assaulting the dominant scientific racism of the time. Nonetheless, the rise of liberal environmentalism in the social sciences is only one side of the story of racial developments in the 1920s, and this modern view of race was confined for the most part to a distinct minority.

These newer intellectual developments must be narrated alongside and in view of the broader social tensions that permeated the culture.[52] The "modern" twenties were also racked by nativism, especially white Anglo-Protestant resentment against the rising influence of immigrants, Catholics, Jews, and African Americans. Many white Americans did not welcome this increasing cultural pluralism and urban diversity. The FCC's theology of brotherhood was being worked out in this social context when competing groups, such as the Ku Klux Klan, attained remarkable growth and public visibility. The Klan's fervent Protestantism and nationalism offered an alternative vision and theology to that of the FCC. The FCC's desire to unite Christians of different denominations and to Christianize and reform the American nation was only one such project among others.[53] As Kelly Baker writes about the Klan: "the order launched campaigns across denominational lines in its efforts to save Americans from immigration and other 'evils.'"[54] The Klan was one of the most active and fastest-growing movements of the early to mid-1920s, combining a powerful and compelling (for many) dedication with an exclusivist vision of a white Protestant nation.

Historians are not accustomed to making comparisons between the Klan and more respectable "mainline" organizations such as the FCC, but the FCC's vision for a Christian America loses some of its historical specificity when we ignore the religious nationalism of contemporary groups such as the Klan. Although the Klan was only one among many groups or movements that held an anti-pluralistic vision of America as a unified white Protestant nation, it was one of the most organized and visible during the 1920s.[55] Its membership peaked at four million in 1924 out of a total population of around 114 million Americans. The Klan claimed chapters in 48 continental states and had a membership comprised of Baptists, Methodists, and Quakers, just to name a few.[56] Like the FCC, the Klan had a detailed plan for and vision about race in America. And like the Klan's theology of exclusive white nationalism, the FCC's theology of brotherhood was crucially integral to its plans to reform the nation. In stark contrast to the Klan's racial vision, the FCC was one (religious) expression of the "cultural gifts" movement of the 1920s, which emphasized the distinctive contributions of immigrants and Blacks to American culture.[57] Attention to the persistence and widespread nature of the exclusivist vision for America highlights the significance of the minority position of the FCC's race relations project and its break from dominant racial theories in the 1920s.

The FCC's various projects against racial injustice were grounded in this theological vision of human unity. For its leaders, deviation from this truth about human brotherhood and unity in the church was more aptly regarded as a "heresy" than incorrect doctrine about the virgin birth or the precise nature in which Scripture was inspired.[58] This vision was being formulated in a moment when debates were raging in the Protestant world over the authority of Scripture, and when conservatives were attempting to drive liberal Protestants from their denominations on charges of heresy and apostasy.[59] While conservative Protestants were more concerned about whether evolutionary theory challenged the uniqueness of humans or whether they had been created in God's image, they displayed little regard for whether racial theories of segregation diminished the value of some human beings (in this case, African Americans and other non-whites). The FCC regarded the true heresy as white supremacy, which placed race as the basis of divine mission rather than grace as the divine gift that all humans needed, regardless of their racial or ethnic heritage. This vision of unity in the church, transcending nationalistic loyalty or ethnic pride, was reiterated in 1934, a year after Adolf Hitler came to power. This "Appeal to Christians of All Lands" urged Christians "to bear witness anew to the God of love who, through Jesus Christ, has broken down the wall of partition between nations and races and summons all mankind to the larger fellowship of the Kingdom of God."[60] It denounced a "self-seeking nationalism" that was manifesting itself all over the world. This theology of brotherhood rejected a narrow vision of Christian witness that gave primacy to racial theories of white superiority. It noted: "We invite the people of the churches of the world to join us in proclaiming anew our citizenship in a kingdom that is without geographical or racial division. At a time when nationalist loyalties are being accentuated, we would call upon all Christian people to bear witness to the imperishable truth that in Christ they have a fellowship that is worldwide."[61] It was this consistent witness against racial bigotry that undergirded the various racial projects of the Department. All the activities described in the following chapters were tied to this central vision of brotherhood and unity in the body of Christ.

2

"A Stain upon Our National Honor"

From the inception of its Commission on Negro Churches and Race Relations in 1921, the FCC pledged to sway churches to speak out against lynching and committed itself to educating the public on the evils of lynching for at least five years.[1] This initial project of education and changing attitudes eventuated in full support of several federal anti-lynching bills and a massive public relations campaign to highlight the atrocities of lynching. The entrenched violent behavior and dehumanizing beliefs of people who participated in lynchings fundamentally challenged the FCC's tendency to rely on publicizing factual information as a primary means of changing attitudes and swaying public opinion. Lynching symbolized the depths of racial oppression in America and indicated how hard it would be merely to get many white Americans to recognize the basic humanity of Blacks. Yet, lynching served as a learning experience for the FCC, alerting it to the depths of racial oppression in America and yet highlighting the necessity of its public pronouncements about brotherhood. The leaders of the FCC were forced in many instances to reconsider the efficacy of their proposals for changing the nation.

In some ways, the FCC's anti-lynching campaign was similar to the work of the National Association for the Advancement of Colored People (NAACP), which had begun its attack on lynching a decade earlier than the FCC, though it was formed one year after the FCC. Both organizations realized the need to change the very language that was used to describe and frame lynching. As Philip Dray notes of the NAACP, "[It] set out to reverse the very language of lynching by emphasizing the criminality of lynchers and those who protected them, and to rub America's face in the gritty business of hanging, shooting, and roasting defenseless human beings."[2] Like the NAACP, the FCC would condemn the American nation for allowing such atrocities to occur, but the FCC had a special message for churches, calling them out for their silence, hypocrisy, and oftentimes for their refusal to address lynching as a crime and moral wrong. Both organizations published massive amounts of material to highlight the barbarism of lynching, and supported federal legislation to end the practice. The FCC was especially interested in goading churches to address the practice. Even so, the NAACP was the leading non-church organization to engage in a public and visible anti-lynching campaign, and commanded greater resources to address race problems as its central reason for existence. The FCC, by contrast, had only one department devoted to racial issues and thus its very organization and limited resources ensured that it would address race as one among many other problems facing the nation. Nevertheless, it was the most prominent religious organization outside of the South and in fact worked with the NAACP, often following its lead or collaborating with it to find better ways to end lynching.

Nonetheless, the public work of this major Protestant interdenominational body lent some respectability to the anti-lynching campaign. After all, President Franklin Delano Roosevelt chose to speak out against lynching at the 25th anniversary meeting of the FCC in 1933.[3] He said, "This new generation, for example, is not content with preachings against that vile form of collective murder—lynch law—which has broken out in our midst anew. We know that it is murder, and a deliberate and definite disobedience of the Commandment, 'Thou shalt not kill.' We do not excuse those in high places or in low who condone lynch law." In contrast, it was not until 1947 that Harry S Truman became the first president to address a gathering of the NAACP, almost a decade and a half after Roosevelt's address to the FCC.[4] The FCC also saw itself in a custodial relationship with its member constituents, finding ways to move them on significant social and moral issues. The FCC tried to exert influence on local church bodies and communicated regularly with the Women's Missionary Council of the Methodist Episcopal Church, South before it threw its support behind the Costigan-Wagner bill in 1934.[5] Given the hostility to the NAACP in the South, even among churches, it can be safely inferred that the FCC's anti-lynching work was an important factor in convincing a number of southern religious leaders to support federal anti-lynching legislation. Not only that, but the vast missionary reach of the FCC and its work in other countries allowed it to communicate statements by leaders in other parts of the world to its constituents, which often contained graphic rebukes of Christianity, with lynching as the primary example of Christian hypocrisy and brutality in America. The FCC shrewdly pushed against segregation and racial violence by labeling them major obstacles to the propagation and spread of the Christian gospel. While its message was not accepted by many churches, its role as a leading Christian organization emphasizing unity in the body of Christ as the visible witness of Christ's work in the world gave some leaders pause when it offered its public pronouncements on the churches' responsibilities in the world. Thus, its anti-lynching campaign was significant for its actual and symbolic impact.

What impact did the FCC's anti-lynching campaign have? The FCC, the NAACP, and other organizations were disappointed in their hopes for federal legislation to end lynching. Yet, the symbolic authority attached to this public face of the Protestant establishment surely was an important advance in the anti-lynching campaign. By using its resources to end lynching, educating the public through many publications, speaking to church leaders and conferences, and engaging in a letter writing campaign, the FCC's work against lynching must be told alongside that of the NAACP, the Commission on Interracial Cooperation (the most prominent southern organization working against lynching in the 1920s), and the Association of Southern Women for the Prevention of Lynching in future general narratives. This Protestant ecumenical body spent over two decades fighting against lynching, and I try to tell this story in more detail than older narratives on Social Christianity. The theology of brotherhood that broke away from a dominant theology of segregation must gain a place in broader narratives of Progressivism,

Social Christianity, and political liberalism, especially as parts of each tradition sought to widen the circle of citizenship beyond Anglo-Saxon white Protestants and envision a more multicultural nation. White Protestant Christians who opened limited spheres and offices to Black leaders and women in their inner circles joined with secular organizations and individuals to take on entrenched evils such as lynching, a development that certainly played a role in the FCC's full-frontal attack on segregation by the late 1940s.

This narrative is not simply a story of historical retrieval, important as that is, but a reminder of how cultural authority wanes and attaches itself to certain groups at particular moments in time. Few today are aware of the FCC's anti-lynching campaign. Historians of American religion are apt to place the FCC within an anemic ecumenical tradition that lost out to evangelicals in the long run, thus succumbing to a teleological narrative of inevitable decline because there was something supposedly inherently defective about the FCC and its bureaucratic infrastructure. In some ways, we are still indebted to the critiques of the Niebuhr brothers (Reinhold and H. Richard) and to a general Christian realist interpretation of the FCC and ecumenical strands of Christianity, which identified these strands as being naïve and hopelessly optimistic in their conceptions of human nature. Yet, these critiques fail to account for the FCC's pamphlets and detailed reports that described at length the brutality of lynching, that stared evil and injustice in the face, calling down judgment upon the nation and the churches for their failure to eradicate this evil. The organization suffered great abuse and criticism for its unpopular stance on lynching, and was drawn into local controversies after enlisting its own investigators to reveal the truth of these atrocities. Racial hatred and violence became powerful catalysts that shook the faith of FCC leaders in America as a "Christian nation" and were factors in developing what David Hollinger calls a "mood of self-interrogation" among ecumenical Protestants.[6] Time and again, lynching was held up as not simply an obstacle to evangelism and foreign missions, but a blot on the nation's character and a stain on its conscience. "How could a Christian nation allow its most oppressed victims to be burned alive?" was a constant refrain in this literature. How could America claim an exceptionalism rooted in Christianity and democratic fairness when Black Americans suffered so cruelly at the hands of white Americans, especially in that part of the nation (the South) that claimed the highest rates of church membership? The anti-lynching campaign not only helped to change the nation, but it was also a factor in altering the FCC's conception of the nation and its churches.

Scholars have argued that the Second World War was a transition point in American foreign relations, when domestic civil rights activists sought to expose the inconsistency of America's war against fascism and the racist policies of Nazi Germany with America's own racial oppression of Blacks. The FCC, with its long international reach and its missionary work, had long exposed this contradiction. Even before the war against fascism, the FCC exploited America's claims of democracy and fairness by pointing to the most brutal manifestation of American racism, the lynching of Blacks. The call to churches to practice brotherhood at home in order to increase their credibility on the foreign mission field was another form of this rhetorical and political strategy—highlighting the nation's glaring internal contradictions over against its image as a beacon of democracy. As historian Mary Dudziak argues, the anti-lynching campaign and the incipient civil rights activism of the 1920s did not lead to "extensive social change", but they did loudly and insistently proclaim that there was a "conflict that inhered in American ideology and practice" fully two decades before the Second World War.[7]

Mob Murder and the Churches

In its first major publication against lynching, *Mob Murder in America: The Challenge Which Lynching Brings to the Churches* (1923), the FCC demonstrated its commitment to a number of ways to end lynching (because of its lack of a strong theoretical definition of church-state relations, the FCC could both support legislation and yet claim it did not *formally* support specific legislation on behalf of its constituent members).[8] First, the shrewd public relations strategy of playing up southern religious leaders' statements on the evils of lynching was put into motion. Three quotations condemning lynching in clear and unequivocal terms were published. All were major addresses from interdenominational gatherings in North Carolina, Arkansas, and Georgia. Prominently displayed at the end of the pamphlet were the names of all the personnel of the Commission on Churches and Race Relations. There were a considerable number of southern religious leaders' names, ranging from places such as Atlanta, Georgia to Orangeburg, South Carolina. The FCC was aware of the fallout from the NAACP-backed Dyer bill, which had been introduced in the House of Representatives on April 11, 1921 to make lynching a federal crime, but was defeated in the Senate by December 4, 1922.[9] The question of states' rights was a live issue, but many southern churches saw the bill as an attempt by outsiders to meddle in their affairs. Thus, the FCC's 1923 book highlighted its southern representatives and the public pronouncements of prominent southern religious leaders. Still, the perception of the FCC as an outsider persistently plagued the organization's attempts to change racial attitudes and practices in the South, and its support of federal legislation created great difficulties in gaining the support of southern religious leaders.[10]

Second, graphic portrayals of the ghastly work of the lynch mob were presented alongside stark figures that indicated the number of lynchings that had occurred in the United States. There were 4,154 persons lynched between 1885 and 1922, the pamphlet grimly noted. Three out of four victims were Negroes. As high as these figures were, there were certainly "many more of whom no record was made [who] were similarly murdered." In 1919, 83 persons were lynched; in 1920, 61; in 1921, 64; and in 1922, "at least" 57.[11] Bleak statistics and numbers were set off against bold news headlines describing the sordid details of a lynching. One example included a Negro looking "on in dumb wonder" while bound to an iron post with logging chains as "stern visaged men" heated pokers and smoothing irons "until they were as fiery as the flames that licked them hot." A mob estimated in the thousands gathered, even as the merry voices of children on the outskirts of the area romped and played. When everyone finally gathered, the violent work began. The mob had allowed the Negro to squirm for half an hour as the pokers flamed red hot; now they were ready to sear his eyes, face, and body. A pile of wood and rubbish was heaped on the body of the Negro victim causing his "agonized body" to squirm and writhe beneath its load. When the fire finally consumed the wood and rubbish, the victim expired, probably welcoming death as a merciful release from his agony.[12]

The FCC dramatized the details of the lynching: the fury and seeming senselessness of the lynch mob as it carried out its organized work of torture. The procedures and tools of torture were also described. One section of the report noted: "Some of the victims suffered indescribable torture, such as saturation of parts of the body with kerosene or gasoline so that they could be burned piecemeal, branding with hot irons, or the gouging out of eyes and ears with red-hot irons." Though "wild and savage," lynchings were planned and deliberately carried out. There was an order, structure, and ritual to these events.[13]

The third notable element of this pamphlet was its specific appeal to churches. The pamphlet began with an indictment: "It hardly seems credible that America, with its *great Christian churches and its missionary enterprises*, its homes, schools and courts, permitted" so many lynchings to occur (emphasis mine).[14] The report was careful to note that one lynching happened on a Sunday morning "not far from two churches." In boldface print, the pamphlet noted that in some cases, "these atrocities have been perpetuated within the sight of churches of the community." Christians must awaken to the fact that mob murder mocks Christian ideals. All Christian profession was rendered hypocritical by allowing such a "savage practice" to exist. It flouted "the very foundation principle of human brotherhood for which the Christian church stands." Here then was the FCC reiterating its commitment to a theology of brotherhood that was fundamentally challenged by the dehumanizing lynching of another human being. The pamphlet raised the stark question of whether Christianity or savagery would rule in American communities. Finally, the problem that lynching posed to the efficacy and spread of the Christian Gospel was raised. It was noted that "its true power to the colored races of Asia and Africa" could never be realized "so long as the very land which sends the missionaries does not itself assure humane and Christian treatment for all its citizens." The "lynching evil" stood as a reproach against "Christian America" in places such as India, China, and Japan, as missionaries and travelers attested. Noted Bengali poet Rabindranath Tagore was reported to have been asked what he thought of America's missionary endeavors in India. He replied, pointing to a newspaper clipping showing that two Blacks had been burned alive in America, "So long as this goes on in your own land, do you think you have any Christianity to export?"[15]

Clearly, the FCC was deeply troubled about the obstacle that racial oppression, symbolized by and enacted most brutally through the practice of lynching, represented to an effective Christian witness. Its project of demonstrating the sufficiency of Christianity could never be even approximated in view of the public dehumanization of Blacks that lynching signified. Yet, the concrete proposals and recommendations of the FCC should also be noted alongside its concern for the reputation of Christianity; the FCC could often appear as if it were using injustices against blacks as a means to some higher end. Notwithstanding its overarching concern for the public reputation of Christianity, the FCC refuted all the common arguments for lynching, agreeing with *all* of the leading anti-lynching arguments going back to the points raised by Ida B. Wells in the late nineteenth century.[16] They noted, for example, that lynchers even took the lives of Black and white women, despite the claims to protect womanhood and motherhood. The pamphlet emphasized in bold print that nearly four-fifths of all lynching victims in thirty-seven years had been killed for alleged crimes other than rape, the principal public justification for lynching in the South. Around twenty percent of Black lynching victims were accused of rape or attempted rape.[17] All of this data was intended to inform the public about the brutal reality of lynching, and to rob lynchers of any moral justification for their actions.

The pamphlet concluded with specific suggestions for measures to prevent lynchings. It called upon states to enact special laws against lynching, noting that though the Dyer bill had been killed by a filibuster in the Senate, some still felt a federal law against lynching should be enacted so long as states refused to curb it. The pamphlet urged more effort by local authorities and courts to capture and convict participants in lynch mobs, even if this required a change of venue to make trials easier. Governors should be given power to remove sheriffs who had proven derelict in their duties, and "a mounted police force" must be provided by the state to local governments to contain the fury of the lynch mob. "Public spirited citizens" must back up sheriffs and prosecutors who performed their duties against the mob and oppose those who failed to do so. Public opinion, especially in the public press and newspapers, must be used to move officers and instruments of the law. The pamphlet noted the powerful role that editorials and news columns played in shaping public opinion and inciting crowds about issues of race.[18]

Included in the FCC's anti-lynching recommendations were several that applied specifically to churches. It reminded Christians that, as voters, they could help to secure legislation against lynching in their local communities. They could contribute funds for competent legal counsel to convict those involved in lynch mobs (specific reference was made to the Commission on Interracial Cooperation in Atlanta, Georgia, the leading southern organization against lynching). They could shape public opinion by influencing local newspapers to take a fair and just approach to racial issues. In their "organized capacity," churches could also hold up the Christian ideal of appropriate relations between the races. That included ministers in the pulpit speaking against lynching and stirring the conscience of their congregations to abhor this form of violence. Churches must persuade people that the "Christian way" of positive goodwill, mutual respect, and friendly cooperation "will really work." They must "impress the dangers of lynching atrocities and their awful effects upon the people, the communities, and the Nation by a distribution of literature against these evils." They should provide educational talks and lectures on Black progress and the "better side of race relations." Conferences and meetings must be held with recommendations on how to prevent lynchings and for formulating plans "to secure the cooperation of all the moral forces of the community or commonwealth." Churches should also observe Race Relations Sundays, a newly created FCC annual holiday held on the second Sunday of February, where Blacks and whites came together to get a better understanding and deeper appreciation of each other.[19] In short, the FCC's recommendations for churches and its suggestions on how to end lynching represented a central part of its project for better race relations.

Rituals of Penitence and Repentance

Religious organizations are known for their rituals. Religious rituals often tell us more about the nature and mission of organizations than their public creeds and statements of beliefs. Prayers, poems, and annual calls for penitence marked the structured rituals of the FCC's Department of Race Relations, especially around the reality of lynching and mob violence. As already noted, the FCC's anti-lynching campaign was launched in 1922, beginning with a study of the problem. Much emphasis was placed on publicizing factual information and changing public opinion. The principal means of doing so was the *Honor Roll of States Free of Lynching*, which was published annually until 1934. In announcing the report each year, George Haynes would document recent trends and note the significance of shifts in public opinion. The *Honor Roll* also regarded and recognized lynching as a national problem and thus made little distinction between southern and other states. By tracing trends and the growth or decline of a "mob spirit," it made reference to the state of the nation and its moral progress or decline. The *Honor Roll* was a way of highlighting or questioning the extent to which the United States was truly a civilized Christian country of law and order.[20]

The *Honor Roll* was a part of the ritualization of the FCC's race work, and reflected its tendency to memorialize and sacralize certain times of the year. Yearly reminders, monthly events, and recurring messages functioned as a way of incorporating what were normally regarded as "secular" practices into the sacred Christian year. The *Honor Roll*, studded with statistics and numbers, was alternately a progress report and an indictment of the nation. It was a yearly reminder of where the nation stood in its ability and willingness to rid itself of this stain upon its reputation. It was a condemnation of the practice of Christianity in the United States. The *Honor Roll* sought to portray a reverse image or perverse inversion of American exceptionalism. America, professedly a Christian nation and a beacon of democracy, allowed its poorest and most despised minority to be tortured, mutilated, and burned alive in the presence and with the active support of thousands of fellow citizens. What kind of nation would allow this level of brutality and violence in its midst, and not hold responsible those who committed such atrocities?

Prayers of penitence seemed fitting in view of the growing problem of lynching. On Race Relations Sunday, February 12, 1928, Haynes released a public call to penitence and prayer, noting the "sobering fact that more than four thousand people have been victims of lynching in our country" and that this fact "has filled all people of goodwill with a sense of horror and shame." He wrote that thirty persons had been lynched in 1926, which almost doubled the number for 1925, a fact that was "so flagrantly opposed to the progress of right and brotherhood that all who are committed to the way of Christ are asked to observe a day of penitence and prayer that our American nation may be purged of this blot upon our civilization."[21] The prayer expressed a desire for a change of attitude; it was a way of viscerally and emotionally identifying with the horror of this brutal act. As Haynes wrote: "In entering into the deep realities of penitence and prayer we take upon ourselves the guilt of those who blindly lead mob violence and the suffering of those who are its victims." An entreaty was made to God, that the "Living God" would have mercy upon the nation, check the "mad passions" that arise within all in the nation, establish moral discipline and self-control in the midst of the nation, teach true tolerance and brotherhood, grant clear knowledge of the nation's failures, and offer a vision of new possibilities. The entreaty concluded that "we may have fearlessness in facing intrenched [sic] wrongs and unflagging energy in striving for a social order permeated by the spirit of love and fellowship."[22]

In offering this prayer of penitence, the FCC returned to its foundational theology of brotherhood. It requested a deeper sense of God's fatherhood and human brotherhood, especially praying for a purging of all false pride of race, all prejudice and suspicion, and all arrogant self-assertion. A deep sense of the precariousness of Black life in the nation and of the fragility of human connectedness was noted in this entreaty, beseeching God "that none may need to live in fear of violence or feel unsafe in his brother's presence, but that the life and liberty of all people may be held sacred and secure." The FCC recognized that the churches' teachings and practices regarding human brotherhood and connectedness would have to be revised and radically transformed. It implored God "that the church of Christ may gain standards of aims and values more in accord with the spirit of Christ, so that it may not merely preach brotherhood but may exert a mightier influence in making it a reality in our daily lives."[23]

In incorporating an entreaty and call to repentance and prayer alongside a frank discussion of the "evils of lynching and mob violence," the FCC immersed itself into the nitty-gritty of human sin and brokenness. The work of the lynch mob—torturing, mutilating, and burning its victims—was narrated in graphic detail in the same release calling for prayer and divine help. No separation of secular and sacred was made here. No claim that this was outside the sphere of the work of the churches. Rather, the release argued, as it had done so many times before, that "every lynching that occurs is an indictment of Christianity before the world." This "savagery unthinkable among civilized people" was a reminder that Americans must "Christianize ourselves or stand condemned in our efforts to Christianize others."[24]

Though it is difficult to know how many in the South actually read releases of the FCC, which were quite widely disseminated in newspapers and in church press materials, the FCC tailored its message specifically to Christians. They highlighted how the United States must have looked to other parts of the world, and how incongruous it was to send missionaries to other parts of the world when people were being brutally murdered by mobs in greater numbers in the very part of the country where Christianity was most widely practiced. Included in these rituals of repentance, then, were indictments of the nation (asking God for forgiveness for "our national sin of lynching and lawlessness," and for this stain upon its "national honor"), and a critique of the Christian churches for their silence and failure to incarnate beliefs and practices that would deprive lynchers of moral justification for their actions. The FCC's work against lynching thus reflected a prophetic strand of Christianity within the ecumenical movement. It was principally a witness against the nation for tolerating evil.

Exploring the Meaning of Lynchings

Department leaders surely realized that their public relations campaign was insufficient to deal with the ingrained culture of mob violence. By the 1930s, the FCC threw its support behind a federal anti-lynching bill and began hiring its own investigators to get a more accurate assessment of the causes of lynchings in local communities. Originally, it had deferred to the Tuskegee Institute and the NAACP for statistics on lynching and its causes, but the longer the problem persisted, the deeper the FCC was drawn into an analysis of the causes and nature of lynching. This had been evident, to some extent. in its very first pamphlet on the topic. But by the 1930s, the FCC was taking a more active and independent stance, becoming more drawn into the local and political controversies that surrounded the practice.

Twenty-two lynchings took place in 1930, doubling the eleven that occurred in 1929. Many people were deeply troubled by this spike, for lynching deaths had been on the decline throughout the 1920s. The year 1930 was a significant development in the anti-lynching campaign. In response to the uptick in lynchings in early 1930, the Commission on Interracial Cooperation (CIC) created its Southern Commission on the Study of Lynching, increasing the effort to gain a deeper understanding of not simply the factual and narrative details of lynchings, but the social and economic factors involved. On November 1, 1930, the Association of Southern Women for the Prevention of Lynching (ASWPL) was formed in Atlanta, Georgia, under the leadership of Jessie Daniel Ames, who was director of the CIC's Women's Division. The International Labor Defense (IDL), a legal advocacy group, commenced its work in the South, having formed its first southern conference in Charlotte, North Carolina, in December 1929. One of its goals was to abolish lynching.[25]

The 1930s represented the culmination of years of reform efforts to end lynching. Most of the leading anti-lynching groups grappled with the need to bring the brutal reality of lynching before the public without objectifying Black bodies and making them the object of a sordid gaze. Detailed investigations became the rage during the Great Depression. In part because of the economic hardships of these years and the particular social and economic problems the South faced, studies of lynching began focusing on the illiteracy, poverty, and cultural stagnation of the South, pointing to them as the root causes of mob violence.[26] But the principal thrust, especially in the efforts to garner support for federal anti-lynching legislation, was to rob lynchers of claims to moral superiority (allegedly protecting "white womanhood") and to reveal lynching as a "most deplorable act of moral barbarism."[27] The FCC's messages to the churches and its changing tactics to get at the truth of lynchings were parts of these developments in the broader anti-lynching campaign.[28]

The most significant development in the FCC's anti-lynching campaign in the 1930s was its employment of investigators, whose findings were often published in the *Information Service*. Usually, these were persons "who had previous knowledge of general conditions in the area," though some were trained sociologists and academics hired by the FCC to conduct a study of the area. These persons were commissioned to investigate the underlying social and moral causes of the lynching and to ascertain what the various constructive forces of the community, especially churches, had done to prevent a lynching or to condemn it after it occurred. Some effort was made to determine discreetly who brought before the legal system the names of those who participated in it. The investigator was also charged with observing the general conditions or relations between the races and the nature of the community out of which the lynching arose. Many of the extracts from these reports were printed in news releases for the local newspapers. These reports evoked passionate responses, especially among local residents who often criticized these "outside" investigations as biased and unfair to their community. In two separate incidents (in Maryville, Missouri, and Salisbury, Maryland), the FCC was brought face to face with the prejudices and constraints of local communities. These experiences with local communities became one of its many confrontations with the tenacity and depth of racial oppression.

A vivid example of the FCC's investigative reporting on lynching was published in 1931 in its *Information Service*, a weekly newsletter of the Department of Research and Education. The Maryville, Missouri, lynching occurred on January 12, 1931. Dr. Gilbert Cox, minister of the First Methodist Church in South Bend, Indiana, who had held a pastorate in Maryville, was chosen by the FCC's Department of Race Relations to conduct the investigation. Cox had also been active in interracial work for a number of years during his pastorates at Columbus, Ohio, Chicago, Illinois, and South Bend. Raymond Gunn, a Black man who was pronounced "mentally defective," had been accused of murdering a nineteen-year-old white school teacher, Velma Colter. After his investigation, Cox concluded that Gunn, who had been previously convicted of an assault on a woman and had served a prison sentence for it, was guilty beyond a shadow of a doubt, mentioning Gunn's confession as only one piece of evidence. Cox presented an unvarnished account of the lynching. He estimated that people came from a radius of forty miles either to witness or participate in the lynching, and that over two thousand whites were present (in a town of five thousand people). Gunn had been chained to the roof of the schoolhouse, which was saturated with gasoline and set on fire. A number of men in the group fired into the burning schoolhouse. A mother held up her little child and said, "Look, honey" as the flames destroyed the schoolhouse. Remnants of Gunn's charred body, in addition to furniture and unburned timber, were carried off as souvenirs. Reports from neighboring towns indicated that mothers had asked doctors if children were in danger of infection from handling pieces of Gunn's bones and flesh.[29]

The editor of the *Information Service* newsweekly wrote that the lynching gave "a terrifying sense of the weak foundations upon which our modern social structure seems to rest." Of the five ministers in the town, only one mentioned the lynching from the pulpit. One minister spoke of the need to "quiet our minds and turn our thoughts to making our lives the best we can," in the hopes of "doing what God would want us to do." The sermon was about Christians giving evidence of the grace of God in their daily living, illustrated by the story of the conversion of a drunkard. What was clear from the FCC's report is that the churches would do little if anything to stop the practice of lynching. But Cox's recommendations were included in the newsletter. He called for a "race relations committee" in every community, where various problems such as crime, housing, and employment could be discussed. A social or medical agency was needed for the "mentally diseased" like Gunn. Changes in the law were necessary to give the governor the power to provide for the security of prisoners in circumstances in which a lynching was likely. Participants in the lynching must be brought to justice. Schools "must teach the consequences of such acts and the churches must show by word and deed that such atrocities under any circumstances whatsoever constitute a betrayal of everything that can be called Christian."[30] Apparently the irony of this last recommendation was lost on the editor, who had just indicated the complete failure of most churches to even acknowledge that a lynching had occurred. For all of its analysis of the social, economic, and historical causes for the lynching, the newsletter's report leaves one with the feeling that whites were determined to carry out this act no matter what risk was involved. After all, it was acknowledged that there was "almost universal sanction of the plan before it was carried out and of the deed after it was done."[31] What confidence then did the FCC have that schools and churches would prevent lynchings in such an environment? This failure to dig deeper and recognize the tenacity and depth of racial oppression was a constant struggle for the FCC, with its tendency to rely on moral suasion, reasoning, and the presentation and dissemination of facts as the principal means of addressing racial problems.[32]

In its investigation of the other incident mentioned above, the FCC found itself defending not only its choice of who conducted the study, but its very reputation as an impartial Christian organization. On December 4, 1931, a lynching occurred in Salisbury, Maryland. Matthew Williams, described as a "mentally defective Negro," after having shot and killed his white employer, tried to take his own life while at Salisbury Hospital. A white mob took him from the hospital and hanged him by a rope in a court yard. Williams' body was dragged by a rope tied to the back of a truck and taken to a gas station. The body was drenched with gasoline, pulled to the section of Salisbury where most Blacks lived, and dragged around the streets before it was set on fire. Williams' fingers were then cut off and distributed as souvenirs alongside short lengths or sections of the rope on which he had been hanged. The FCC hired Professor Broadus Mitchell of the Department of Political Economy at Johns Hopkins University. Mitchell's study was an attempt "to discover the conditions in the community which made a lynching possible and the effects of the lynching upon the attitudes of citizens." He interviewed more than a dozen Black and white residents of the area, including the chief of police, the county sheriff, the mayor, the nurse in charge of the staff at the hospital from which Williams was taken, and two ministers. Mitchell concluded that the Chesapeake Bay's cultural environment contributed to the lynching and that the "geographical isolation" of the Eastern Shore region of the state left it in "rather backward conditions." Making an argument about the distinctiveness of the region, he argued that the area had become "backward in its moral and spiritual development."[33]

Mitchell especially noted that he was struck by the public justifications and "excuses" for the lynching, made fully two weeks after it occurred. No one from among the intelligent and fair-minded citizens exerted any significant effort to stop the lynching, even though he granted that "some ignorant townsmen and countrymen" were responsible for carrying out the lynching (two citizens made some effort to stop the mob). The chief of police, his three patrolmen on duty, and the sheriff and his deputies offered no resistance to the mob, and it was known in the town an hour or more beforehand that a lynching was likely. Mitchell wrote: "The impression was received by the inquirer [that is, Mitchell] that the public spirit of Salisbury is far below what is desirable. Those whom one would expect to be leaders in a crisis decided to fall in with the ignorant, the prejudiced, the frightened, the sullenly boastful." To be sure, he claimed that few leaders had remained in the community and many of the ablest young men had left the region for employment and other reasons. After chiding the city for its "lack of civic morality" and its weak "public spirit," Mitchell recommended an "active local interracial committee."[34]

The Reverend George W. Dawson, pastor of the Centreville M. E. Church, rejected the conclusions of Mitchell. Dawson called the FCC's report "ridiculous and absurd." He argued that the intellectual capacity and moral responsibility of Salisbury citizens were as good as anywhere else in the United States. For him, the report brought disrepute to the FCC's Department of Race Relations. Others accused the FCC of acting outside its realm and without the full facts. Few if any of these reports had much to say about the lynch mob and virtually no condemnation of the townsmen for conducting the lynching.[35] In a letter dated March 17, 1932, the FCC's administrative committee wrote to Mitchell that despite the fallout and criticisms of the report, they stood with him. Though they were "severely criticized" in certain quarters, the leaders of the

FCC expressed gratitude for the work Mitchell had done. Nonetheless, it seems a bit odd that the FCC asserted that it did not feel that a public statement of support was necessary. If some were not only denying the report's validity and publicly raising doubts about its "official authorization" by the FCC, then surely it deserved some public comment from the FCC. Mitchell was asked if he had seen the March 10 edition of the *Salisbury Times*, which claimed that the FCC had repudiated Mitchell's report.[36] Though the FCC later expressed its endorsement of the report in a letter to the *Times*, it would appear that some vocal public support of Mitchell and a clarification of his being authorized to write the report were necessary. So troubled was the FCC by all the ruckus created by the report that it tightened its policies on selecting investigators of lynchings. In a meeting held in New York City in April 1932, it was emphasized that great care must be taken in selecting the person to conduct such studies (a virtual concession to criticisms of Mitchell), making it necessary to get the prior approval of the chairmen of the Race Relations Department, the Administrative Committee, and the Policy Committee of the FCC. Public statements and the actual results of the study were to be given extra scrutiny, and would have to go through a more rigorous internal examination.[37]

Perhaps the FCC felt it had not done enough homework on Mitchell. Critics accused Mitchell of suspect associations. Newspaper editorials and ministers sought to link him with the American Civil Liberties Union (ACLU), which they regarded as a Communist organization.[38] The *Salisbury Times* editorial stated: "It is not easy to understand why any member of the Federal Council of Churches would employ a man noted for his Socialist leanings to investigate and report upon a community where more than 90 percent of the white inhabitants are active church members or have a stated religion reference, except that the Council did not know the type of man they were assigning to this mission."[39] In reality, it mattered little who did the investigation. Criticism of the townspeople for their participation in and justification of a lynching, here and elsewhere, invariably evoked heated criticisms of "outsiders" and debates about biases of the investigator and the motives of those sponsoring such studies. Some asserted that prejudiced and violent Communists were using these reports to stir up animosity between the races.[40] Surely, others asserted, only proponents of federal legislation that would restrict states' rights would be interested in these issues.

Not only did critics attempt to delegitimize the findings of the FCC and who they chose to conduct these kinds of studies, but they cast aspersions on the organization as being out of touch with everyday church people—as an organization that did not appreciate or understand the practice of Christianity among local folk. This led not simply to rebuttal in the form of a valorization of the alleged hospitality and openheartedness of the people of Salisbury or some other local community, but a disregard for the substance of the findings and hardly any reflection on the reasons such a violent mob act would occur, except for occasional passing references that the event was unfortunate. What often followed was a theological critique of the FCC as having an inauthentic or misguided religion, and a regional critique that it was an elitist New York organization that wanted to make local people look bad.

No matter how hard it sought to partner with organizations such as the CIC and the ASWPL, the FCC could never quite successfully shield itself from these criticisms when it became more actively and locally involved in the campaign against lynching. Its very attempt to learn the mores and practices of a local community inspired criticisms of it as an outside meddler. This was all the more painful for the FCC because it billed itself as a representative Protestant organization that worked on behalf of all denominations, regardless of their location. As an ecumenical strand of Protestantism that emphasized Christian unity, it hoped to heal the rifts among major Protestant bodies, especially those that had developed among Baptists, Methodists, and Presbyterians over slavery. Contrary to the claims of local critics, in reality the FCC exerted great effort to work alongside and defer to local church bodies and pastors, but active support for its race projects was simply weak in the South. It was forced to accept the fact that the problem of lynching would never be solved if left solely to southern and local authorities and churches. Federal support would be needed.

The Fate of the Campaign for a Federal Anti-Lynching Bill

Although the FCC did not formally support or endorse the Costigan-Wagner bill introduced in 1934 (or any of its following variations), it was in general support of federal legislation to criminalize lynching. Its many years of anti-lynching work made it clear that southerners were not going to address the problem without outside pressure or coercion. In fact, as all of its own reports indicated, vocal support for many lynchings was not lacking on the part of southerners, and its investigations of the local customs that fostered and bolstered the practice, rooted in a system of racial segregation, led increasingly to a broader critique of segregation in the South and racial oppression in the entire nation. Even so, the anti-lynching campaign often took attention away from the deeper nature of racial oppression in America by looking at its ugliest manifestation. Lynching was such a visibly and notably barbaric practice that, by the 1930s, it was increasingly defended only by white southerners rehashing old arguments about sexual assault and chivalry—arguments that had been discredited by the leading anti-lynching groups decades earlier (and conclusively rebutted by the ASWPL in the 1930s). Yet anti-lynching measures were easier to elicit support for than a frontal assault on segregation and the everyday slights that Black people endured in the South. Economic and political oppression received some attention from the Department of Race Relations, but it was only after the federal anti-lynching campaign stalled that greater attention was focused on the broader interlocking system of US racial oppression. Nonetheless, the anti-lynching campaign was an education in the limitations of public pronouncements, and it schooled the FCC in the difficult and messy work of soliciting support for legal and political change, especially through the tedious and slow-moving legislative process of the national

Congress. Only with the help of these allies would the fight against racial oppression make any substantive progress.

Quietly, the FCC ended its *Honor Roll of States Free of Lynching* in 1934. Apparently, because lynching was spreading to states outside of the South, it was deemed pointless to highlight an honor roll. The anti-lynching campaign had acquired an array of new players who made this honor roll seem antiquated, even though for insiders and for its educational goal of changing Christians' attitudes, there was always a ritual dimension to the honor roll, calling the nation to account, reminding Christians of their moral duties, and lamenting wanton destruction of Black victims and praying for divine justice for the lynch mobs. Was the FCC ashamed of its *Honor Roll*? Given the public visibility of the anti-lynching campaign and the involvement of so many prominent groups, it seems that the FCC was more self-conscious about the perception of the *Honor Roll*'s efficacy, given that lynching was spreading to more states. One can only speculate, given that not much discussion surrounded its quiet ending.

The ending of the *Honor Roll* coincided with much more active work on behalf of federal legislation, and a public relations campaign to get Christian churches to throw their weight behind the renewed assault against lynching. In a hearing before a subcommittee of the US Senate's Committee on the Judiciary on February 20, 1934, Samuel McCrea Cavert, general secretary of the FCC, testified about the work of the FCC against lynching. Cavert noted that the though the "educational effort" to end lynching was under the direction of the Department of Race Relations, the FCC "as a whole has again and again given voice to its deep conviction that the prevalence of lynching in the United States is a black stain upon a civilization that is called 'Christian.'"[41] Perhaps anticipating the criticism that it was pointless to award an honor roll, he stated that the FCC was appalled to discover that there were only five states left with no lynching record, indicating that lynching had spread to more states by 1933 than in any of the eleven years since the honor roll system began. Cavert reminded those gathered that, of the recorded 1880 lynchings between 1900 and 1930, there were only twelve known cases in which a conviction was secured. This was conclusive proof that state and local authorities were not adequately dealing with the problem. After listing a number of church bodies that had condemned lynching, he indicated that the FCC had called Christians "to penitence for this national sin" and demanded more vigorous and effective legislation against lynching. This amounted to tacit support of a federal bill.[42]

As with Cavert's testimony before Congress, Department leaders made public and private efforts to get churches to support local and federal bills against lynching. Pamphlets and publications continued to be part of the educational effort to change attitudes and alert church people to the evils of lynching. Cavert signed a letter sent by the NAACP to President Franklin Delano Roosevelt, US Attorney General Homer S. Cummings, and Governor David Sholtz of Florida, protesting the lynching of Claude Neal in Marianna, Florida. The letter requested enactment of a federal anti-lynching law, investigation of the liability of lynchers under a kidnapping law, and indictment and prosecution of the guilty in light of the investigation.[43] The FCC carried on extensive correspondence with southerners about the Marianna lynching, in an effort to garner support for its attempts to secure prosecution of the lynchers by Attorney General Cummings. Additionally, on November, 3, 1934, a statement about the Marianna lynching appeared in the *Information Service*.[44]

Letter writing, public gatherings and marches, and public and private efforts to gain support for legislation to end lynching on the local and especially the federal level increased throughout 1934 and 1935. National politicking in particular assumed a greater role by 1935. The FCC sent a letter to interracial committees and key people across the nation, asking that letters be sent to President Roosevelt and their senators to resist a filibuster of the anti-lynching bill before Congress. Telegrams were sent to southern women in particular, requesting that they repudiate South Carolina Senator "Cotton Ed" Smith's defense of lynching as "necessary for protection of womanhood."[45] Katherine Gardner, an associate secretary in the Department of Race Relations, not only made a special trip to Washington, DC, to observe the debate on the anti-lynching bill, but probably expended more efforts to end lynching than any other member of the Department. As a white woman, Gardner's working alongside George Haynes, an African American, was intended to model the FCC's interracialism in action (which was especially notable in view of an oft-repeated justification of lynchings). She wrote letters to church bodies, sent out fundraising letters, tried to persuade church women (especially on women's committees of various denominational boards) to make anti-lynching a priority, wrote letters to the editors of magazines such as *Christian Century*, the *Nation*, and the *Survey* to highlight the tragedy of lynching, and worked alongside the NAACP by helping to coordinate joint meetings and marches to garner support for anti-lynching.[46] By 1938, Gardner was on a first name basis with Walter White, executive secretary of the NAACP.[47] Her work was a major force in the FCC's efforts to end lynching, and she was a key person in presenting detailed information on lynching during the meetings of the Department of Race Relations. Her work, and that of many other women behind the scenes, corrects older scholarship that focused primarily on the work of white men in the internal dynamics of the FCC, especially in the less public or "respectable" work of race relations as opposed to foreign policy and international goodwill issues.[48]

Though the FCC and other organizations did not succeed in getting Congress to pass a federal anti-lynching bill, they did much to publicize the nature and extent of lynchings. Throughout the next ten years, the FCC continued to point to the hypocrisy of Christians who professed peace but allowed this form of brutal violence as a "solution" to alleged instances of violence against whites. Lynching challenged the FCC's faith in the nation and compelled it to critique the churches for their failure to come together and eliminate this national problem.

Yet, leaders of the FCC could point at the end of 1946 with some relief to the creation of President Harry S. Truman's Committee on Civil Rights as partial vindication of their campaign. When the committee submitted its report, *To Secure These Rights*, to the president on October 29, 1947, the FCC could claim a partial victory in educating the public about violence against Blacks and in its call for a federal anti-lynching bill. On November 18, 1947, the Executive Committee of the FCC, in an official resolution, called *To Secure These Rights* "a notable contribution to our progress toward a working democracy." It recommended the report to "all church people" for careful study and reflection. The resolution argued that it was the special "responsibility of and opportunity of churches to promote discussion of the Committee's report within the framework of the Christian understanding of our faith in God as revealed through Jesus Christ, as it is related to our social living." The FCC commended the president's report for attending not only to the distinctive issues facing Black Americans, but "also to other racial and religious minority groups within our society." While the FCC acknowledged that there could be honest differences of opinions about implementation of some of the recommendations of the report, it focused particular attention on the report's support for the protection of human life (part of the FCC's continuing concern about the scourge of lynching); equal opportunity for employment, without regard to race, religion, or national origin; the ending of segregation "in all its aspects, including the outlawing of restrictive covenants in real estate contracts" (the FCC also passed a concurrent formal resolution against racial restrictive covenants); and the right of "every adult citizen" to vote.[49] The resolution concluded by recommending that churches take the report seriously, but also by emphasizing its international implications. It noted that the nation's struggle for "true democracy cannot be isolated from the world scene." The FCC's resolution emphatically noted: "We cannot hope to influence other peoples to accept the Christian way of life, or other nations to accept democratic principles we proclaim unless we can demonstrate in our own community living that we take them seriously and are striving to translate them into effective practice."[50] The broader ramification of race relations in the US was a theme to which the FCC would return again and again as a tactic to shame the nation and to goad it to live up to its democratic ideals.

Given the moderate style and tenor of the president's report, the FCC's resolution makes sense in its approval and commendation. The report opened with a forceful assertion of the essential "right to safety and security of the person," depicting "lawless violence" and "arbitrary arrest and punishment" as key threats to such a right.[51] In a style similar to that of over two decades of FCC pronouncements, the President's report tallied the number of lynchings that had occurred since the 1920s. It deplored the fact that too many Black Americans still lived "under the harrowing fear of violence or death at the hands of a mob or of brutal treatment by police officers."[52] The report's theory of social change was similar to the FCC's model. It argued that legislation and education must work together to eliminate prejudice and intolerance, that education was a "means of improving civil rights," and that private organizations and individuals should help to educate and shape public opinion. However, the report insisted, though it may be impossible to overcome prejudice solely by law, "many of the evil discriminatory practices which are visible manifestations of prejudice can be brought to an end through proper government controls."[53] Its concluding remarks on lynchings turned to their lasting impact and their national and international repercussions. The worry that lynchings would tarnish America's international standing was a version of the FCC's longstanding claim that they were a stain on the moral soul of the nation. The report put it this way:

> A lynching in a rural American community is not a challenge to that community's conscience alone. The repercussions of such a crime are heard not only in the locality, or indeed only in our nation. They echo from one end of the globe to the other, and the world looks to the American national government for both an explanation of how such a shocking event can occur in a civilized country and remedial action to prevent its recurrence.[54]

While it is true, as these words indicate, that the Cold War led to a heightened concern with the US's moral reputation over against the claims of international Communists about universal brotherhood transcending color lines, the FCC's anti-lynching campaign shows a much longer record of using American race relations for international purposes and to shame the nation before an international audience.[55] It is thus not surprising to see the FCC supporting Truman's report and its strategy for civil rights, which mirrored the vision held by the FCC.

Small victories were celebrated in the long fight against lynching. The fight continued through the 1940s and beyond, mostly by public calls for federal anti-lynching bills. But perhaps just as important was the realization and claim that witness was central to the church's mission, even if influence could not be tangibly measured. Lynching stood as both the real and the symbolic evil that had to be opposed, and for which the nation and its churches must be held accountable. Though sometimes it was a voice crying in the wilderness, the FCC cried out long enough that it was joined by other religious partners who had once eschewed this kind of difficult work. In this regard, the FCC could see some measurable results in goading and pricking the conscience of some churches, though its attempts to change attitudes and uproot old customs remained an uphill struggle.

3

Race Relations Sundays

In July 1937, George Haynes spelled out what he believed to be the crux of the interracial problem in the United States. After briefly discussing the history of slavery in America, the development of economic, social, and political inequality in the US, and the rationalization of racial prejudice and discrimination against Blacks, Haynes turned to his present moment and argued that the "uprooting of old evils and customs that new conditions have made intolerable and changing the inferior-superior attitudes are among our greatest national problems."[1] He believed that altering "the practices and conditions of everyday relations between white and Negro people" was essential to modifying these inherited customs and attitudes. For Haynes, practices preceded ideas and attitudes. Even so, he argued that they worked in a circular fashion: "As we change the practices of everyday relations, our ideas and attitudes will change; and as our inferiority-superiority customs and attitudes are modified they effect changes in our everyday practices."[2] Thus, for Haynes, relations or relationships were at the crux of altering the interracial problem in America.

Haynes noted that there were areas of everyday life where race relations had become fixed in past generations and therefore required specific attention in order to be changed in the present. These included relationships on farms and plantations, in industry, in politics and civics, and in religious institutions. Although the FCC's Department of Race Relations targeted all of these areas in some form, Haynes gave special attention to churches, which had a "unique function and opportunity to deal with this basic interracial situation."[3] This emphasis on concrete personal relations and practices distinguished Haynes's program to modify accumulated customs and attitudes of racial discrimination and prejudice. His brainchild, Race Relations Sunday, was a central part of his project to realize racial brotherhood within the churches and to undermine persisting racial prejudices among Christians.

Race Relations Sundays were held once a year beginning in 1923. Yet, important as it was, Race Relations Sunday was only one plank in achieving the goal of improving race relations, supplemented with interracial clinics (workshops, beginning in 1943), local race relations committees in cities, and national conferences (in addition to the national anti-lynching campaign). Race Relations Sunday was also the major holiday in the FCC's calendar and part of its attempt to sacralize the secular year with new holidays that supplemented traditional Christian holidays.[4] There was an explicit and implicit liturgy in these holidays. They incorporated Christian brotherhood into the very worship and practice of the church year. They regularly reminded Christians of their communal identity as people from all races committed in their common worship of one God revealed through Jesus Christ, who broke down the artificial barriers that formerly separated them. These holidays also included rituals of repentance, confession, and calls for divine judgment, reminding the nation and the people of God (Christians) that mob violence and racial oppression were blatant assaults upon the ideals of Christian brotherhood and equality in the family of God. In this way, Race Relations Sunday (and its accompanying celebrations and holidays) stood as the FCC's central tool to realize Christian brotherhood in churches and to (re)sacralize an old Christian year that now required explicit reminders and affirmation of equality in the body of Christ.

George Edmund Haynes: The Power of Relationships

From the first meeting of the Department of Race Relations, Haynes called for multiplied "opportunities such as conferences, meetings and committees for personal contacts of white and colored men and women" with the hope of gaining "confidence in each other."[5] This emphasis on developing trust between the races reflected a strong belief in the power of personal relationships. Given the number of Americans who went to church (compared to their numbers in other organizations) and Haynes's belief in Christianity as a divine source of personal and social change, he argued that it was within the "walls and cloisters of the churches [that] the ideal of brotherhood may be fostered in those who will go forth to challenge the *practices*, to preach the ideals of the future divine events, and to teach true science and *new techniques* to misguided America. The Christian religion carries the Great Dynamic for this social change" (emphasis mine).[6] What gave Haynes confidence that Christianity could eliminate the barriers between the races, despite the dominant theology of segregation in the South and the reality of de facto segregation in most churches in the North? A simple answer is that he truly believed that there was a power and hope inherent in the Christian message and way of life. It was an act of faith consistent with his understanding of Christianity. Haynes maintained a sanguine view of personal and social transformation through Christian practices throughout his public career. His biography and educational experiences also help explain the particular form that Haynes's arguments took, though there is always an element of biography that remains elusive to the historian. One can only cull the clues from Haynes's experiences as an African American growing up in the segregated South, and from his years in several prominent universities and organizations before his active work in the FCC's Department of Race Relations, in order to shed a partial light on why he believed certain practices were crucial to changing attitudes and social customs.

George Edmund Haynes was the major figure in the development of the theological underpinnings and the actual work of the FCC's Department of Race Relations. David Wills rightly argues that Haynes and Benjamin Mays were two of the most influential African Americans within the inner circles of the Protestant establishment before the emergence of Martin Luther King, Jr. on the national scene in the 1950s. Haynes was the first African American to hold an executive position in the FCC, when he became the executive secretary of the Department of Race Relations in 1934. Haynes and Mays were present at the special meeting of the FCC in Columbus, Ohio, in 1946, when its historic endorsement of desegregation was announced.[7] When he stepped down in 1947, Haynes could look back with some gratification at the growth of a host of innovative projects that he had instituted.[8]

Haynes was born in Pine Bluff, Arkansas, in 1880. His mother was a domestic worker and his father a laborer. After graduating at the top of his class from Fisk University in 1903, Haynes went to Yale University, studying sociology with William Graham Sumner until 1904. The following academic year he studied at Yale Divinity School. After spending two summers (1906 and 1907) as a student at the University of Chicago, then doing graduate study at the New York School of Philanthropy and traveling Europe in 1910, he found time to enroll at Columbia University, where he received a doctorate in 1912—the first African American to do so. A man of enormous energy, Haynes was employed at a variety of jobs, working as the secretary of the colored men's department of the International Committee of the YMCA from 1905 to 1908, and then, from 1910 to 1920, he was professor of sociology and economics at Fisk University. After a two-year stint as Director of Negro Economics at the United States Department of Labor, he helped form the National Urban League, and for a short while was its executive director. It was the publication of Haynes's *The Trend of the Races* (1922) that brought him to the attention of the FCC's leadership and its newly formed Commission on Negro Churches and Race Relations.[9] Perhaps because of its optimistic tone and its lauding of white missionary and philanthropic efforts among Blacks in the South, this book made Haynes an appealing choice for leadership in the FCC's race work.

In hindsight, *The Trend of the Races* served as a blueprint for Haynes's work at the FCC's Department of Race Relations. It set forth his diagnosis of the problem of race in America and his proposal for addressing that problem. Although Haynes became actively involved in political and economic issues (after all, he had worked in the field of economics), the book indicated his tendency to address issues that he regarded as more fundamental than laws and politics. As he wrote:

> The machinery of government and law can do a great deal. Attitudes and the habits of thought and action of both individuals and groups, however, lie back of government and control the machinery of the law. While regularly looking to the law, therefore, the two races have to establish those relations which crystallize into law and which make customs and governments.[10]

This argument—about the settled attitudes and customs from the past persisting in the present and continuing to exert a powerful influence on contemporary life—was the most consistent one that Haynes articulated. It also shaped the remedy he proposed. It was not that he distrusted legal remedies or had a distaste for political activism (though the failure to get Congress to pass a federal anti-lynching bill would indicate all too clearly the limitations of outright political and legal action); rather, Haynes felt that laws rested on deeper attitudes, feelings, and practices. To these he directed a great deal of attention. Unless these attitudes, feelings, and practices were altered, Haynes argued, new customs, laws, and attitudes could not emerge.

This emphasis on attitudes and habits has often been judged by critics as a distraction from deeper economic and structural inequalities. Yet it does not appear that Haynes neglected these economic and broader social concerns in his implementation of policies to change racial attitudes. But this particular focus did indicate the direction in which most of his energy would be channeled. Haynes expressed this attention to attitudes in a comparative sense in the following statement: "Through all the chapters and implicit in every section of this book is the theme that the relations of the two races finally rest, not upon wealth or poverty, not upon things or lack of them, but upon the mental, social, and spiritual attitudes and habits of conduct that grow out of the feeling experiences of the two races as they have contact in agriculture, industry, education, government, religion, and the like."[11] This clearly put Haynes at odds with Socialists, Communists, and other reformers who argued that economic inequality and exploitation lay at the root of racial inequality in

America. To be sure, he argued that it was "very difficult, if at all possible, to divide the problems of race from economic problems."[12] Haynes traced contemporary attitudes and practices toward African Americans to the past of slavery, when white Europeans sought "cheap labor" by enslaving Africans. He argued that with the rise of the cotton economy, "profits made out of the business silenced or warped the humanitarian and the religious conscience of the majority" and served as a defense of racial slavery.[13] Thus for Haynes, the past refusal to treat Black Americans as human and the exploitation of their labor were foundational to current white American attitudes and practices toward Black people.

Haynes noted that "some of the most intense race friction" occurred in industry, when blacks and whites encountered each other. Later, he developed a keen interest in the problems of black farmers and the economic hardships of black sharecroppers in the Deep South. Nevertheless, Haynes attended to and hoped to alter attitudes, feelings, and customs, which he felt could in part be done by pleasurable "feeling experiences" in which the two groups could meet on a regular basis. His objective was "that the ideals of Jesus may determine the conditions of these experiences and the conditions of their contact."[14] That is, his hope was that the relations between the races in the future would be grounded in the ethics of Jesus. Haynes was convinced that African Americans in particular would, if given the freedom and opportunity to do so, "show America and the world a new meaning of Christian brotherhood."[15] They would bring a "distinct and rich contribution to the larger life of America," and white Americans had no reason to fear the full development of their cultural, political, social, and economic life. While not a utopian vision, Haynes offered a sanguine Christian social theory in which fixed and accumulated patterns of racial contacts were altered by interactions of good will, mutual understanding, and tolerance. The immediate goal was to provide such repeated pleasurable experiences.

In a social context in which Blacks and whites were becoming increasingly segregated into separate neighborhoods, churches, and social networks, Haynes called for cooperative endeavors that would bring the races together to achieve common goals and share common projects. He rejected the dominant philosophy of "social Darwinism," which placed the struggle for existence at the center of human life. Haynes believed that this kind of thinking, where life is seen as a social struggle of all against all and physical force is the guiding principle, was what led to the First World War. He pointed to recent scientific research indicating that the "mutual aid principle" was widespread among lower animals. New research also indicated that humans' "higher social virtues have their roots" in a factor of "otherism" which, Haynes said, suggested that "impulse toward such mutual action is as fundamental in nature and in human nature as the tendency to struggle in conflict against each other."[16] This joining of the most recent findings in social science with historical and theological emphases on human brotherhood was the foundation of the FCC's race relations project as articulated by Haynes.

Haynes felt that there was "almost unlimited opportunity for promoting racial cooperation" through organizations like the FCC's Commission on Churches and Race Relations. He saw schools, churches, home and family life, government, and voluntary organizations as "avenues through which pleasurable contacts may be made that create new attitudes and ways, [and that] give the spirit of brotherhood the opportunity to operate."[17] Haynes was emphatic that, if Blacks and whites were to come together in these ways, whites would have to realize that they were not simply working *for* Blacks, but *with* them as partners. Each race's destiny was bound up with the other's welfare. To support these positive and pleasurable contacts between the races, Haynes proposed popular forms of education, which he termed "propaganda." Newspapers and different organizations would be enlisted to stress "racial likenesses," instances of good deeds, and more positive reports of each race. He was certain that whites needed more instruction than Blacks, given that "Negroes know the life among white people better than the latter know the inner side of life among Negro people."[18] The press, the pulpit, the lecture platform, the "moving picture," and conferences and conventions would therefore be crucial as avenues of "educational propaganda" in altering negative views and stereotypes, particularly those regarding Blacks. One example that Haynes was careful to stress was the white press, which played such a crucial and sometimes deadly role in inciting white mobs to violence and lynching. Timely news and fair-minded editorials, he noted, could save lives and prevent violent racial clashes.[19]

It is striking that each of Haynes's proposals rested on the willingness of Blacks and whites to create such interracial contacts. This assumption, paradoxically, was founded on his faith in the power of such contacts. Haynes was deeply impressed (and apparently indelibly affected) by William Graham Sumner's notion that social groups responded to pleasurable and unpleasurable experiences, and that the experiences of one group or generation could become habitual and thus take on the nature of a social force for future groups and succeeding generations. The terms that Sumner used and the ways in which he described the evolution of folkways left a deep impact on Haynes's views of social organization. Although Sumner was deeply suspicious of social reform or engineering, his major work, *Folkways* (1906), which Haynes drew upon repeatedly for categories and conceptual notions, did allow for variation and growth in folkways and customs. The following brief analysis of Sumner's massive work is not intended to be comprehensive, but rather a summary of the central concepts and ideas that shaped Haynes's thought.

The central insight in Sumner's work is that folkways are produced by the "frequent repetition of petty acts."[20] These repetitive acts become habits in individuals and customs in groups. Over a period of time, these habits and customs rise to the level of a societal force, exerting a strain on every individual within its range. Another way that Sumner puts this is to say that "men begin with acts, not with thoughts." Actions motivated by some compelling interest or need move humans forward in their quest to satisfy that need. This focus on action was Sumner's way of indicating that thoughts, secondary reflections, and philosophical analyses had little place in primitive societies and arose later as second-order contemplations of the world. What guided humans in their actions at the crudest level were the avoidance of pain, which constrained various acts; and pleasure, which served as an impetus to further acts or experimentation.[21]

Sumner's grand structure of how societies are formed, how folkways become mores, and how various customs change under new conditions impressed itself on Haynes's mind, and created the general contours of his own social theory of how prejudice and racial stereotypes were formed. Sumner's emphasis on the formation and tenacity of customs, traditions, rituals, and suggestion as powerful forces that shape human behavior all had a profound impact on Haynes. Haynes's tendency to place action at the center of altering human customs, and his sometimes easy dismissal of ideas as epiphenomenal to behavior, reflected a residual imbibing of Sumner's ideas.[22]

For Haynes, it was crucial to create opportunities for interracial cooperation that would hold the promise of becoming a social force that in turn would become habitual in the life of a people.[23] Haynes argued that negative racial attitudes produced flight from a person or racial group, and that aggression against individuals or groups developed out of "unhappy experiences." These experiences were recounted and handed down in conversations and in writing, especially in the popular press. Memories were passed on to children, and to adults who did not have the original experiences. Thus, hostile attitudes, behavioral patterns, and customs were formed in succeeding generations and became fixed over time. Haynes believed that attitudes of a "friendly nature and cooperative behavior patterns" could arise from happy experiences to disrupt the old patterns. Then memories of these positive experiences could be passed on to future generations. In time, neighborly and friendly attitudes and behavioral patterns would become customary among formerly antagonistic peoples.[24]

That Haynes articulated this theory of the origins of racial inequality as late as 1941 indicates the persistence of the influence of Sumner, whose ideas he had first studied nearly three decades before. Because he kept searching for ways to supplement the annual Race Relations Sunday, Haynes must have realized that such infrequent and small-scale events would face an uphill battle to become major social forces and therefore habitual in the life of a people. Even if one could define these yearly events as pleasurable experiences—in a strong and robust sense of persisting influence and widespread diffusion—one wonders if they were sufficient to transform folkways, given the almost staged nature of the events themselves, which allowed those present just by their infrequency to go back to their default position on race relations. This emphasis on interpersonal relations could easily lose sight of broader inequality, though Haynes's actual work and proposals indicate that his attention to interpersonal relations did not hinder him from addressing structural racial inequality.

Before looking at the means by which Haynes and others pursued these goals, I would like to revisit Haynes's specific articulation of his theology of brotherhood and inclusivity. Much of this theology has to be put together from disparate sermons and messages separated by time and location. It was never systematically set forth, in part because the FCC relied on occasional sermons and gave priority to practice rather than abstract theory. Though the FCC did not have a singular voice, Haynes's writings and speeches serve as representative, especially since his public messages (with the exception of his books and articles) were never solely his own, but the result of the collaborative work of secretaries, fellow clergy members, and other leaders in the FCC.

Haynes argued that, in the family of God, all of God's children are equal. The church must hammer home those Christian values and truths that are opposed to the racial superiority myth. The democratic community that is the church knows no superiors or inferiors. The church must seek through word and deed to rid itself of hostility toward, suspicion of, and exploitation of any racial group. The church must ceaselessly fight against the "modern heresy of race and class divisions." Haynes was insistent that these Christian values should be "repeated through all the means of religious education for the children, the young people, and the adults." Teaching of these values was not simply to be an "intellectual exercise but also an emotional experience of mass contact of the races" to replace old, unfriendly attitudes and feelings.[25] The church must proclaim the infinite worth of each human being and the equality of all, not simply those in the church. It must stand in solidarity with the oppressed outside its ranks. Finally, "original Christianity" agrees with science, democracy, and common sense, which converge on one conclusion: humans must be treated as human beings, not assigned labels of "superior" or "inferior" based on race, birth, or color. Many of these ideas were gathered up in an official statement of the FCC in 1946, in which it asserted that segregation was a violation of the Gospel of love and human brotherhood.[26]

Defining the Plight of Black Americans

In some ways, Haynes's theories seem curious as the musings of a trained economist and social scientist. It is hard to place his ideas within any of the dominant theories of his day about how to tackle the racial oppression that afflicted all African Americans. In the 1930s, the NAACP, the nation's leading African American civil rights organization, was engaged in an ideological battle with the Communist party over race and class. Communists ridiculed the NAACP for its alleged focus on narrow class interests and for failing to address the struggle of most Black Americans. The NAACP criticized Communists for proposing the creation of a separate Black nation in the South, something they saw as a disastrous capitulation to white supremacists. The Communists, in turn, felt that the NAACP's fight for political and civil liberties, while laudable, was not challenging the fundamental economic inequality under which most Blacks labored. Communists, and the leaders of the National Negro Congress (formed in 1936), chided the NAACP for its faith in the Democratic and Republican parties, neither of which, in their view, protected Blacks from disfranchisement, lynching, and the deprivation of their human rights.[27]

This was a debate over the fundamental nature of racism and the most effective and lasting way to uproot it. These theories of social change rested on different conceptions of the human person, placed different emphases on the ways that racial prejudices formed, and offered different means of removing racial oppression. Haynes proposed a combination of techniques and practices, drawn from the social sciences and Christian social teachings. One proposal was internally focused on the churches—Race Relations Sundays. The other was outwardly focused on local communities—the interracial clinics and workshops that sprang up in the 1940s.

Race Relations Sunday: Sacralizing the Secular Year

Race Relations Sundays were based on the idea that *relations* would bring about changes in people's minds and attitudes. Haynes did not have much use for offering at length an alternative to dominant theories of racial superiority, though he did seek to refute them in most of his published works that addressed these topics directly. He didn't theorize at length because he believed that racial prejudices, "frictions, fears, suspicions, and antagonisms cannot be attacked in the abstract and in general."[28] Concrete relations and "pleasant experiences" during the "regular go of things" in everyday life must take place. Only such positive experiences could uproot hostile feelings, prejudiced beliefs and attitudes, and unfounded fears and groundless suspicions. His plan was to bring Blacks and whites together in a non-threatening environment where they could show respect and appreciation for each other.

By attending to "race relations" instead of rendering the problem of race as a stationary Southern or Negro problem, and by refusing to subscribe to dominant notions that racial prejudice is instinctual or natural, Haynes was a pioneer in the emerging, more dynamic sociological conception of race.[29] His *The Trend of the Races* (1922) was a clear break from prevailing social science notions of racial prejudice as instinctive. In fact, Haynes had no use for notions such as a racial temperament, which posited intrinsic emotional and psychological differences between Blacks and whites, a view that even Robert E. Park, a leading sociologist at the University of Chicago, held as late as 1919. Park is known for his race relations cycle theory, which was first articulated in 1921, but developed more fully in his later writings. Park was primarily interested in demonstrating that Blacks could be assimilated into American society; his theory proffered that *race relations* went through four distinct stages: contact, competition, accommodation, and assimilation. Even so, Park apparently believed as late as 1928 that Black-white relations were only in the accommodation stage and the principal obstacles remained Blacks' skin color, their temperament, an instinctive white racial prejudice, and the failure of the races to maintain primary contacts (as opposed to conflictual, "frontier," or distant contacts). This conception of Black obstacles rendered his theory more static than dynamic.[30]

Haynes's concept of race relations not only rejected a static approach, but rested on a notion of "cultural gifts," where Blacks and other ethnic groups contributed distinctive but necessary qualities to American society that made for a richer nation. This contrasted with a one-way conception of Blacks merely assimilating into a dominant white culture and shedding their perceived "peculiarities." The very thrust of his book was to illustrate that Blacks had made many contributions to and sacrifices for the nation. To the extent that Haynes referred to a "race problem," he named it "so-called" and described it as involving the "problems of Negro progress" in economic, educational, social, and religious realms, and in achieving Black citizenship. What he meant by problems were obstacles to Black progress. The real problem he labeled "the problem of attitudes and habitual action of the white world."[31] In spite of these problems, Haynes was convinced that Blacks and whites could work together for each other's "mutual advantage." Nothing about instinctual forces inhibiting progress made their way into this work, though Haynes clearly acknowledged the obstacles to positive relations between Blacks and whites.

At the time when Race Relations Sunday was developed by Haynes, there were few positive interactions between Blacks and whites. The South was rigidly segregated, and the Northeast and Midwest had just begun adjusting, in mostly violent terms, to the influx of Black migrants from the South. The Red Summer of 1919 witnessed race riots throughout the nation, with Chicago and other cities experiencing a huge loss of life and destruction of property. Lynching, often accompanied with sadistic and public rituals that dehumanized Black victims, was now national news, as the NAACP urged Congress to make it a federal crime. Segregated neighborhoods began spreading in the North, and churches were almost wholly segregated in much of the North and South. Some of the gory rituals of lynching involved the handling of mutilated and burned body parts by white participants and observers, some of whom held on to charred knuckles or teeth as souvenirs. Thus, relations between Blacks and white Americans were often violent and dehumanizing, with Blacks trapped in a system of white supremacy that punished Black bodies that did not conform to its dominant ideology of Black inferiority.

Whatever deficiencies one might, in hindsight, find in Haynes's rather optimistic view of relations between Blacks and whites, the dismal nature of race relations at the time he inaugurated Race Relations Sunday and other projects must be kept in mind. Though clearly Haynes's theory of racial contacts was indebted to Sumner and thus extrapolated from sociological theory, Race Relations Sunday was a particular application of this general theory to churches. The hope was to encourage interracial cooperation and positive relations among churchgoers through activities including pulpit exchanges, in which Black pastors preached in white churches and white pastors in Black churches; promotion of liturgies that emphasized unity in the body of Christ and the worth of all individuals; and music festivals, sometimes interracial, that highlighted the artistic contributions of different peoples, but especially those of African Americans. Interracial workshops and clinics were spin-offs from Race Relations Sundays and developed more extensive conversations and publications about interracial cooperation. This was the general thrust of the FCC's Race Relations project: to promote interracial cooperation and develop more opportunities (besides the annual Race

Relations Sunday) within and among churches for discussions and joint projects related to racial issues.

The first Race Relations Sunday was celebrated on February 11, 1923. It was promoted through churches, the Young Men's Christian Association (YMCA), the Young Women's Christian Association (YWCA), and social agencies as a chance to "come together in pleasurable contact so that friendly emotions and attitudes might be aroused and hostile or unfriendly emotions and attitudes prevented or replaced."[32] It was held on the second Sunday of February to bring it close to Abraham Lincoln's birthday, but its public announcement indicated that its appeal was primarily to "religious motivation," though a frank acknowledgement stated that "the patriotic motivation" was also utilized for its first few years. In announcing the second observance of the day, the first printed pamphlet of "Suggestions and Material" recounted the vast movements of people in the United States, especially Blacks and whites, the crowding of Blacks into industrial towns and cities, the restlessness produced by the World War, lynchings, memories of past frictions, sufferings, prejudices, and a "danger of racial clashes." The pamphlet noted: "All this comes as a challenge to the churches to promote the ideals of brotherhood, mutual understanding, goodwill and the methods of cooperation."[33] These racial divisions and violence were regarded as an opportunity for the churches to offer an alternative to dominant conceptions of race relations. The pamphlet continued: "On this second annual Race Relations Sunday, we, who profess to be lovers and followers of the Prince of Peace, may very properly and wisely assemble to recount to each other our allegiance to the ideals of cooperation between the races. On this Day we should become better informed, each race about the other, and be inspired for greater effort in spreading this gospel of goodwill." Spreading a gospel of goodwill through various means and venues, recounting its adherence to the ideals of cooperation, and helping the races to become more informed of each other through concrete contacts and more accurate information were all ways that the FCC would use its Race Relations Sundays to promote better race relations for the following decades.

The FCC began by utilizing informal cooperation with groups such as home missions societies of various denominations, the YMCA, the YWCA, churches, and interdenominational groups to promote Race Relations Sunday. But the office of its Department of Race Relations gradually became a "national clearing house of information," with its own plans and suggestions for the promotion of the holiday, though an informal group of denominational representatives met occasionally and acted as an advisory board. Leading newspapers gave prominent space to these celebrations of racial harmony. Letters from local church federations and councils provided general information about how the day was observed, as a way to spread its reputation. Yet, from its inception, there was variation in the way that participants received and interpreted the idea of Race Relations Sunday. While the FCC's Department of Race Relations provided general guidance on the conduct of the event, it unfolded differently from place to place. Reports of observances in 1924 came from localities as widely separated as Chicago, Illinois, Little Rock, Arkansas, and Los Angeles, California. Some of these reports on the day were rather general in their descriptions of what happened. Generalities of the following kind were published: "Many newspapers published editorials and extracts from the leaflet (suggestions for observance) beforehand; white and colored churches exchanged choirs. In cities like Dayton, Ohio, and Kansas City, Mo., special joint interracial mass meetings were held. In Chicago, through the guidance of the Chicago Church Federation, six Negro pastors exchanged pulpits and related the experience afterwards."[34]

Often, quotes from ministers who attended these celebrations were printed. One example from the Chicago area in 1924 follows: "A white Baptist minister said: 'It gave me personally a better understanding of the problem that I had previously had. It also could not help but soften the prejudice of the people present. Will be glad to repeat the experiment again.'" According to this same report, a "colored Baptist minister" stated after he exchanged pulpits with a white minister, "Had the finest kind of time over there. Never spoke to a more cordial audience. At least fifty persons came forward after the service and shook hands with me."[35] Sometimes, the reports were not so laudatory and told the story of failed attempts. In 1926 in Gary, Indiana, a city with a large population of Blacks because of the steel industry, local leaders were unable to sell the idea of a general observance of "Interracial Sunday" because of opposition from Black and white ministers, with the primary resistance from Reverend F. W. Backemeier, a white minster in the local Presbyterian Church. Eventually several ministers got together and held an interracial gathering in First Methodist Episcopal Church, led by Dr. W. G. Seamon, a white minister. This gathering was described as a "very excellent and almost spectacular evening meeting." The local leader who sent this report to the FCC noted: "At this occasion there were numbers from the choirs of the respective churches closing with a chorus of the three united choirs which was quite effective. I am enclosing a program for you. We had thought it a good plan to interview separately and individually each minister, white and colored, and get his personal reaction to this business of Interracial Sunday. By the way, Dr. Seamon promises to make this an annual demonstration in his church."[36] Seamon was known for his downtown ministry and his work among African Americans in the city.

Although local contexts continued to celebrate the day in slightly different ways, the FCC's Department of Race Relations began using this day as annual national forum to preach (through radio and in major church pulpits) about its ideals of goodwill and brotherhood. February 12, 1928 was marked by a "Call to Penitence and Prayer," which focused on lynching and mob violence as "a national crime which leaves its stain upon us all." These prayers seemed fitting in view of the ritualized nature of Race Relations Sunday. These liturgical moments became central to the identity of the Department of Race Relations. Yearly events of this sort supplemented a Christian calendar deemed sorely deficient in its attention to brotherhood and racial unity. A report was sent out on June 1928 to over 1500 correspondents, calling their attention to plans for the next observance of the holiday. The hope was to pay particular attention to "the Mexican situation in the United States and the American Indian problem," which were to be "played up equally as prominent as the white-Negro relationships." One report observed: "Problems of relations between white and Negro people grow more pressing upon the churches year by year. A recent report on American Indians disclosed conditions which should arouse Christians. Mexicans are increasing in numbers in the West and the Southwest. Other racial groups in America present problems for mutual attention."[37] Though this was not the first reference to minority groups beyond African Americans, this broader conception of minority relations was one indication of the FCC's developing theology of brotherhood, which was concretely applied to specific circumstances each year as preparations were made to celebrate Race Relations Sunday.

By 1940, Race Relations Sunday was celebrated alongside Interracial Brotherhood Month (the entire month of February). The annual report for that year noted that the day was "designed to bring people of different racial groups together for fellowship—in churches, in discussion groups, at dinners and luncheons, in meetings for community betterment." It stated that through the "interchange of pulpits, choirs, speakers, etc. these groups learn more about one another and through fellowship develop attitudes of friendliness and understanding to displace those of hostility and race prejudice."[38] This was the classic Haynes's rationale for these yearly occurrences. Blacks, whites, and other minority groups suffered from ignorance of one another partly because they did not know one another. Misconceptions and inherited racial prejudices could only be cured or addressed by repeated exposure to one another or through personal relations that would presumably help to dispel these hardened attitudes and feelings. This conception of the origins and persistence of racial prejudice rested foundationally on a notion that ignorance because of the absence of contact lay at the root of racial prejudice, and that concrete and personal encounter would dispel these prejudices. It seemed to imply parity between Blacks and whites, and said little about power and enduring hostilities that may not be so easily amended by personal contacts. Besides its failure to address power differences and other factors that related to racial oppression, this theory of interpersonal relations seemed rarely to acknowledge its principal limitation: its infrequency. How could such limited and infrequent occurrences erode sedimented feelings and deep customs that took decades and centuries to develop? Was Haynes simply hoping for the best, or accepting what was available under difficult circumstances? It is hard to tell because Haynes never made public any serious doubts about the efficacy of his projects or the coherence and validity of his theories.

The report for 1940 claimed that "practically all Protestant denominations" supported Race Relations Sunday and that its scope was nationwide "with an increasing interest each year from southern colleges and among young people everywhere."[39] It also stated that the FCC issued on Race Relations Sunday a "special message and program material for use among all age groups in churches and organizations."[40] In specific cities and states, various activities were observed. Chicago's Mayor Edward J. Kelly followed "his custom" of proclaiming officially the date February 11 through the 26th as Race Relations Month and called for "the stressing of goodwill and understanding among all racial groups in Chicago." Over 40 churches in Chicago exchanged pastors with churches of a different race on Race Relations Sunday. Chicago's Civic Federation sponsored a series of panels, round tables, and talks over radio stations, "culminating with a large interracial conference with prominent local and national speakers on the theme, 'American Democracy vs. New Racialism.'"[41]

Other cities and states had their own celebrations. Ohio's council of churches continued its second annual series of interracial dinners and group discussions in about twelve cities, with Black, Jewish, and other speakers appearing before large audiences. South Bend, Indiana, held a symposium on "the problem of races," which "engaged the interest of Negro, white and Jewish groups." In Richmond, Virginia, First Baptist Church, a white church, opened its evening service to an interracial gathering. It reportedly received a "large response" from the white community and even featured singing by the choir of Virginia Union Baptist, a leading Black college. The report indicated that this evening service program "was given at an earlier service of young people on which Chinese, Jews, Negroes and Indians were represented." At a Black Baptist congregation in Brooklyn, New York, a communion service was held. They hosted a white congregation that formerly occupied the building. The white minister preached and the Black minister preached (one can imagine the novelty of a Black pastor serving communion to whites in some of these contexts). In Pasadena, California, an interracial group called the Scattergoods celebrated the event with participation of Filipinos, "Orientals" (the general term used to refer to Japanese and Chinese Americans), Indians, Mexicans, and African Americans. Even interdenominational and interfaith observances occurred. In Gary, Indiana, a citywide banquet was held in which Roman Catholic, Greek Orthodox, Russian Orthodox, Jews, Blacks, and "Evangelical Protestants" participated.[42] It was estimated that about 10,000 churches throughout the country engaged in the observance of Race Relations Sunday. And true to the FCC's function as a kind of clearing house, the memorandum indicated that the Department of Race Relations would "supply program material helpful for any time of the year to churches and communities working for better race relations."[43]

These local events were reported on extensively by the FCC and local newspapers. But their impact is difficult to assess. One illustration of the difficulty is the official report on the seventh annual observance of Race Relations Sunday, February 12, 1939. The report was divided into various sections according to the type of effort that was being put into the project. It was broken into sections on literature, publicity, and a financial statement. What is notable is the disproportionate space given to literature, especially leaflets to disseminate the central message of Race Relations Sunday. A total of 102,000 pieces of literature were printed, ranging from the message of Race Relations Sunday to supplemental material on the children's service to be designed for this season. Channels for distribution included church federations, local interracial committees, YMCAs at colleges, Black colleges, ministers contributing to the FCC, denominational social action committees, and public meetings and conferences. The largest channel or medium of dissemination was through ministers who contributed to the FCC, which suggests that the problem of "preaching to the choir" probably was a real one. Even so, the varied channels of distribution demonstrated that this was a sophisticated enterprise with a keen self-awareness about ways of getting its message across.

The next section of the report, publicity, indicated various forms. Editorials appeared in church journals, and articles appeared in papers (mostly church-related), while secular newspapers and news associations asked for specifics about the day and printed basic summaries of their observance. For the 1939 observance, a race relations message was delivered on NBC and CBS radio for thirty minutes, and local radio stations in Chicago and other areas also carried some aspect of the program.

The financial report has little value because it does not indicate how expenses for Race Relations Sundays compared to other projects.

Local observances were held in most states, with New York holding eighteen, Ohio and Pennsylvania eleven each, and only one in places like Mississippi and Colorado (no real sense was given about why some places held so few meetings, though one can imagine that Mississippi would not have welcomed this inclusive theology of brotherhood).[44]

Measuring the influence and impact of these events is a difficult matter. In all the reports on the places at which Race Relations Sundays were held, there are mostly generalities such as, "An official of the <u>Indianapolis</u> Church Federation [underlining theirs] reported 'the most outstanding observance of Interracial Sunday in its history,'" or "In Chicago there were nearly 50 pulpit exchanges and a dozen special broadcasts." Oddly, the numbers game of tabulating how many attended or participated became a way of measuring success, though the ostensible goal of the project was to alter fundamentally human relations and lessen racial prejudice. No mention was made of what happened on these issues, though one must grant that it was difficult if not impossible for the FCC to measure a change in racial attitudes in concrete terms, in the context of churches where persuasion was the only tool it had to wield. It was quite frankly much easier to add names and numbers, such as the list of those on the *Honor Roll of States Free of lynching* or the number of pastors who exchanged pulpits on Race Relations Sunday. It was simply far easier to tick off several fewer lynchings as a sign of progress than to spell out how literature dissemination and preaching on interracial brotherhood had changed attitudes and brought about new persons and more just structures within churches. That remained the central challenge of Race Relations Sunday: not to define its reason for being (though that required a great deal of thought and theological reflection), but to demonstrate results and show what success looked like in churches. For the most part, numbers and news blurbs were settled on as signs of life and growth in the churches. They multiplied friendly and harmonious interracial contacts, and by Haynes's reckoning that was a good sign (and his theory held out hope that this would have long-term consequences for the future). One has to look beyond the internal reports of the FCC to determine what influence might mean—and that would be a separate though related project. After all, the FCC often partnered with local or state church federations who implemented the projects that it suggested. In these instances, the actual working out of the details of a specific plan of action was no longer the work of the FCC, though it should be credited with having provided information, impetus, and a theological rationale for the project.

Nonetheless, Race Relations Sundays were the most visible and well-known holidays of the FCC. They therefore require some further analysis, however difficult it might be to measure their impact. As a yearly recurring ritual for the churches, they made their way into the Christian calendar, thus acquiring the status of a sacred holiday. Through them, the FCC was able annually to disseminate in a most visible way its beliefs about brotherhood, not merely in abstract form by teachings and writings (though there were many of those), but by fostering a special moment in which Blacks and whites (and other ethnic minorities by the late 1930s) could come together and acknowledge their common Christian heritage and unity in the body of Christ. Though constrained by segregated neighborhoods and churches, for this time of year a small number of Christians could imagine and perform a different kind of reality in which division and white supremacy did not reign supreme. The theology of brotherhood that undergirded these practices was thus given a brief hearing in the midst of a dominant theology of segregation.

The FCC's Race Relations Sunday was one among multiple civic and religious projects to foster racial harmony and religious tolerance amidst growing anti-Semitism, racial hatred, and the threat of totalitarianism. The National Conference of Christians and Jews (NCCJ) launched Brotherhood Day in the early 1930s, which expanded to Brotherhood Week by 1939 and became a national holiday, especially widely observed after the attack on Pearl Harbor in December 1941. The NCCJ argued that Americans were united by a common belief in the "Fatherhood of God and the Brotherhood of Man" and sought to foster civic cooperation and the diminishment of ethnic, religious, and racial prejudice. The NCCJ was part of the larger goodwill movement that had emerged in the 1920s, and the FCC was a key institution in nurturing and working alongside these organizations that emphasized both national unity and the necessity of brotherhood over against the rise of European totalitarianism. Race Relations Sundays served as ritual occasions to both critique the nation for its failure to live up to its ideals of fairness and equality and to goad the nation toward racial, ethnic, and religious cooperation, a recurring theme in the ecumenical strand of Christianity represented by the FCC.[45]

On the cover of its February 11, 1940 publication, which was the annual (eighteenth) observance of Race Relations Sunday, there is an image of a cross to the left of four men walking side by side. The four men from right to left are African American, Asian American, Native American, and white/Caucasian. The cover is labeled Race Relations Sunday, marking Interracial Brotherhood Month. This was the FCC's visual depiction of racial groups walking in harmony as they all looked upward to the cross (which appeared as if it were in the background or off in the distance). The official message for this observance was delivered by Reverend Philip Cowell Jones, associate pastor of the Madison Avenue Presbyterian Church in New York City. Jones chose Ephesians 2:13–14 as his central text: "But now in Christ Jesus ye who sometimes were far off are made nigh by the blood of Christ. For He is our peace who has made both one, and hath broken down the middle wall of partition between us." Jones also included the following selection from Robert Frost's poem, "Mending Wall": "Before I built a wall I'd ask to know/What I was walling in or walling out,/And to whom I was like to give offense./Something there is that doesn't love a wall,/That wants it down." He noted that God's "still small voice" was telling Christians that though millions were being called to arms and death, they should allow brotherhood and peace to prevail in their hearts. Jones wrote, "With penitence for racial bitterness and the lack of social justice in our country, we must begin by eliminating indifference, greed and injustice from our individual lives; then we shall be able to make the Church more representative of our Lord's attitude and purpose." In his emphasis on "all true Christians" faithfully persisting in efforts to make the spirit of Christ prevail in the world and in their personal lives and in his charge that they can then "fulfill their obligation to make the United States of America a nation in which brotherhood prevails," Jones articulated concisely the FCC's dual-edged approach to race. Christians should attend to racism in their hearts and attitudes and within their churches and become an individual and collective source of racial brotherhood in the nation.[46]

But the message included more than a setting forth of a theology of brotherhood. Concrete suggestions were made that should "find expression in changing our social attitudes and practices." Among these were the following: "The Church is called upon to purify herself of the great modern heresy of racial discrimination within her own walls." "Discrimination in industry based on color, creed, or national heritage must end." "Lynching and mob violence must be wiped out." "Inequitable administration of all forms of social security on the basis of racial differences must be prevented." "Hospitals, libraries, parks and all public facilities should be available to persons of all races." Following the list of suggestions, Jones called upon Christians to "conquer hate with love." After stating all of these suggestions and theological arguments as the bases of Race Relations Sunday and Interracial Brotherhood Month, he concluded: "No day or week or month, however, will suffice. Education in brotherhood is a continuing process. We must emphasize Brotherhood Years, Brotherhood Decades, Brotherhood Centuries, until, in the grace of God, it is Brotherhood *Now*."[47]

Although Jones' message was prominently featured first in this FCC publication, the message was followed by practical suggestions for local churches (as in all of these publications): hold music festivals, emphasize the artistic contributions of different peoples, create and present dramas regarding the problems minorities faced, and encourage interracial cooperation in community enterprises. In many instances, booklets prepared for Race Relations Sunday included additional material such as books for children on various groups such as Indians, Mexicans, "Orientals," Jews, and Negroes.[48] Music and hymns were suggested or recommended, usually those that emphasized unity in the broader church that transcended race or locality. Stories, especially designed for children, were encouraged. All of these publications comprised a virtual worship program for local churches, an alternative liturgy to shape and form a different racial sensibility in the churches. Though particular Scriptures and explicit theological statements enfolded racial brotherhood as integral to Christian living, these resources of the Christian tradition were also fused with the most recent literature of the social sciences that rejected scientific racism. More often, the FCC "translated" this more academic literature (at the hands of skilled staff) in such a way that children and others could acquire a more accurate knowledge for and appreciation of the cultures of different minority groups and non-white peoples. It was a process of re-education through worship and liturgy.

In sum, Race Relations Sunday represented the official public witness of the FCC's theology of brotherhood. It disseminated new ideas, encouraged and fostered new relations, and brought Christians into contact with the findings of the social sciences in a way that some perhaps were not aware of or may not have accepted if they had not been adapted to the context of Christian teachings. This contextual nature of Race Relations Sunday messages was clearly articulated in a publication that contained suggestions for building a program in race relations for young people. It was written while the Second World War was raging and made indirect reference to the racist policies and actions of German Nazis: "What shall young Christians do? First, they should remember that they follow a Syrian Jew, whose whole life was given to the breaking down of barriers that separated man from man, and man from God. Second, they should teach and preach and practise His way, interpreting in terms of modern American life His belief that 'All ye are brethren, and one is your Father.'"[49] Interpreting Christian teachings on brotherhood "in terms of modern American life" remained the central thrust of Race Relations Sunday teachings. It was the FCC's service to the churches and its primary tool of offering an alternative liturgy to help realize racial unity in the body of Christ.

4

The Church in the World

Growing out of local interracial workshops in various cities and sporadic and experimental attempts at bringing Blacks and whites together to address various social problems, the interracial clinics emerged in 1944 as the Department of Race Relations' formal program to address the conflicts taking place in urban centers across the country. The immediate impetus was the massive influx of Blacks and whites (and other minority groups) into war-related industries in urban centers. With the Second World War raging and the defense industries scooping up workers at a rapid pace, racial tensions and riots broke out across the nation, with especially violent ones occurring in Detroit and Harlem during the summer of 1943.[1] Here again, as with the race riots that followed the First World War, new thinking about how to address racial conflicts developed.

Haynes, who was responsible for the origins and design of these clinics, argued that they were not lectures or discussions. They were plans of actions to address the social ills of racial prejudices and hostile behavioral patterns. They were self-surveys conducted by local leaders, with the help of experts, to gather facts about problems in their community. Haynes stressed that the clinic was "the *beginning* of a process *aiming to end in social action*" (emphasis his).[2] The clinic was a technique, an action plan that would be followed up and carried out by those in the local community. Its purpose was to assist representative leaders of the religious, social, labor, business, and civic organizations to share their knowledge and experience, through a community study, in dealing with interracial relations in such matters as housing, education, and recreational activities and to formulate a consensus on what can and should be done to improve the conditions in that community.

The "clinical technique," as it was commonly called, became such a frequently used tool of the Department of Race Relations that a whole literature grew up around it. Manuals were prepared. Articles were written to describe its origins and implications.

As with the rationale for Race Relations Sunday and the effect of relations or concrete contacts between different racial groups, Haynes was the main theorist. In 1946, he published an essay, "Clinical Methods in Interracial and Intercultural Relations," in the *Journal of Educational Sociology*, which articulated the rationale for the clinics that the FCC had been sponsoring for one year. Haynes noted that "civilization can only survive by placing the contacts of races, classes, and nations upon a reasonable, brotherly basis" because modern means of communication had made the world into a "narrow neighborhood." He stated that the contacts between the various groups are "grounded in everyday situations," which are in turn entered into by individuals and groups who have been "conditioned by different religious beliefs, by family habits, [and] by various ways of doing things." Thus problems of "major adjustment between individuals and groups are created by these contacts."[3] Haynes argued that often people will channel their frustration at scapegoats rather than accept that their fears might be because of personal failures or mistakes. Minority groups can become targets in this process.

Haynes labeled the attitudes and fears that accompany the problems of adjustment between different groups "mental phobias." The clinical method was a step toward "eradicating the mental ills of fear, suspicion, stereotyped ideas about other peoples and cultures—through the application of confidence, understanding, and good will across racial and cultural lines, which produce *mental health*." The language of mental health in part was used because this piece was published in a professional journal, but it also represented a growing tendency by the FCC's Department of Race Relations to borrow the language of the social sciences (Haynes also referred to these problems as "mental-social ills"). In any case, Haynes laid out the principal role of the clinical method, which aimed "to enlighten and orient those who have to meet local problems, to enable them through face-to-face analysis of the situation to reach a consensus of judgment on *what to do and how to do it*."[4] He argued that local leaders must be willing to face the facts, especially those pertaining to local employment, housing, schools, religious barriers, and leisure-time. Haynes recommended the "case method" as the best way of ascertaining facts because it attended to local problems as they arose in everyday relationships and in the neighborhoods and communities where people lived and worked. He wanted to avoid over-reliance on generalizations. Only after the facts had been accumulated and faced can a diagnosis be offered. The diagnosis served as the basis for deciding what could be done about the problems in the community and what was the most effective way to go about this.[5]

Haynes had another reason for penning this article: to defend the religious basis of the clinical approach to social change. He argued that religious "leaders were the first social scientists." They had historically recognized and emphasized the social and moral nature of human beings. Through "knowledge, wisdom and revelation" religious experts had sought "to apply the dynamic of the inner, emotional, personal growth to social life." The clinical method sought a sound foundation in science and religion by acknowledging what both had to say about civilization. Haynes was concerned that too many people were adopting a materialistic philosophy of life and refusing to see that civilization has "both a material-physical and a mental-moral-spiritual basis." He tried to demonstrate that a "humanitarian-religious" drive existed alongside other drives and desires in local communities. This could be cultivated with economic, political, and intellectual-artistic drives. Though humans were property owners and wage earners and necessarily existed as economic beings, they could not "live by bread alone." To be sure, they often sacrificed wealth for power, and they aspired for "aesthetic and intellectual satisfaction." Granting that humans strove and fought for wealth, material goods, and power, Haynes nevertheless insisted that moral and "religious desires and aspirations have been powerful forces in every civilization since the dawn of history." These religious and moral desires and drives had given rise to entire movements, organizations, and institutions.[6] This history and this understanding of human society undergirded the clinical approach to social change. It offered a more capacious notion of the human person than a materialist philosophy would grant (Haynes felt that Karl Marx's "materialistic interpretation of life and history" had gained wide acceptance) and argued that religion could be a motivation for humanitarian activity and positive social reform.

Interracial clinics were part of the "national strategy" of the FCC's Department of Race Relations to address the social ills of various communities in the US. By 1945, the Department had a "well-worked out plan" for interracial clinics in seventeen cities in Indiana, Illinois, New Jersey, Michigan, Ohio, Oregon, and Washington. Interested parties were brought together from various groups and constituencies: religious leaders, social workers, business leaders, and members of organized labor. Blacks, whites, Japanese-Americans, Mexican Americans, Filipinos, and Chinese Americans were among the different ethnic groups involved in these face-face-consultations. The FCC usually provided the initiative and the expertise for these local community workshops. Haynes reiterated that they were one step in a long-term process and that all of them required follow up and "some form of permanent interracial council or commission."[7] From the FCC's perspective, the purpose of these clinics was to put in place preventative measures that would forestall or hinder the development of racial violence, but more importantly, create an atmosphere of mutual respect and cooperation among the various groups in any given community. As a technique or tool, it was hoped that the "enthusiasm and zeal of Christian ideals" could be "combined with the technical methods of the sciences" to solve local problems. Haynes felt that there was "tremendous goodwill resources in the agencies and organizations of the community" that could be mobilized for constructive, positive action. Helping communities identify and utilize those resources was the responsibility of organizations like the FCC. The clinical technique then was a concrete way for churches in particular "to apply their profession of Brotherhood."[8]

The Clinical Technique: Interracial Workshops

What did these interracial clinics look like? How were they implemented? And is there any way to measure their success or accomplishments? As with so much of the work of the FCC, the latter question is the most difficult to answer because of the way in which local groups took over projects initiated or sponsored by the FCC. But a general description of the implementation of an interracial clinic in Youngstown, Ohio, in 1945 and a reflection on some of its findings the following year prove illuminating. Youngstown was unique in that it had a long history of an interracial committee, which had "twenty-two years of experience in developing goodwill and democratic practices" by 1945.[9] In the early 1940s, the city was especially facing a problem of housing shortage and racially restrictive practices against Blacks moving into certain areas. Youngstown was also a major source of steel production and thus suffered all the usual competition for factory jobs. The FCC's Department of Race Relations in fact had assisted in organizing this interracial committee in the early 1920s (one of the first so organized by the Department). Several other organizations sponsored the clinic, including the Catholic Diocese and the local bishop, who led the worship service of the first session, the Mahoning County Industrial Council, connected with local industries, the Jewish Federation, and the local federation of churches. Haynes, in his 1946 report on "successful interracial clinics," noted that there was a "marked atmosphere of democracy and eager interracial teamwork apparent with participation of religious, industrial, social and community agencies that sponsored the clinic."[10] There were also a number of out-of-town consultants, including L. Howard Bennett of the American Council on Race Relations, based in Chicago, Illinois, and Marcus W. Collins with the National Conference of Christians and Jews, based in New York City, among others.

Some two hundred persons served on the fact-finding committees of this interracial clinic. Several recommendations were made, relating to housing, schools, hospitals, welfare agencies, and leisure time activities. A call for promoting housing for all low-income groups was made, alongside a demand for assurance of "minimum standards of health, safety, and decency in housing" for all the people of Youngstown. There were efforts to combat restrictive covenants, unfair financing practices, and other restrictions based on "race, creed, or national origin." Attention was directed to teacher representation "based on qualifications without regard to population percentages and without regard to religion or national origin." The implementation of these and many other recommendations was left to a permanent organization created within the Youngstown Interracial Committee.[11] This eventuated in an "Interracial Goodwill Committee," which was chartered in May 1946 with a membership of hundreds of individuals and organizations that paid dues to the group. This council had a board of directors of thirty-six elected members, some of whom were among the city's leading business and professional people. They raised $7,500 by membership fees for the first year's budget.[12]

Haynes's official report on this interracial clinic as a "successful" one just one year after its origins indicates both the limits and the benefits of utilizing the FCC's documents and internal files as source material on how these clinics worked. We get a sense of the scope of involvement and the various groups who partnered with the FCC to effect change in these local communities. Haynes's summary noted that a "well-worded program of action on housing, employment, leisure-time activities, health, etc." was crafted to address the very real problems of Youngstown. As he stated in his philosophy of the clinics, these were action plans and not merely genial conversations without a definite program of implementation. Haynes also pointed out that the clinic was "striking in the commendations it voted to some of the departments of the city government, notably the Board of Education, for democratic and Christian policies and practices."[13] But this emphasis on soaring Christian rhetoric was one of the chief problems with the FCC's approach to local problems. Haynes had little to say about what had been concretely changed in this local community. Although it would be too cynical to suggest that the

FCC hardly cared about what happened, given its time and investment in these projects, still it is notable that the FCC, even with a few local people involved, indicated that it had essentially done its part by providing the expertise. Its advertising of its part and its signaling of interracial work were often seen as sufficient to demonstrate that successful interracial activity was taking place. Haynes, in particular, got caught up in excitedly detailing the varied activities and interracial projects sponsored by the FCC. Too often their mere existence was treated as evidence enough of progress. Only rarely was there acute self-reflection on the need for sustained and long-term effort to alter entrenched prejudices and local customs of discrimination.

Although not entirely the work of the FCC, the very planning of the Youngstown clinic demonstrates the shortcomings of these interracial clinics. Judge Robert B. Nevin, the presiding clinic chairman, sought to dampen expectations by stating about the first meeting (which was held in Trinity Methodist Church in Youngstown): "The purpose of the clinic is comparable to that of a health clinic. We are promising no cures. We shall merely diagnose the sources of trouble, if any, and a board of experts shall then discuss ways and means of curing these ills."[14] Experts diagnosing the illness of the community and making their recommendations as to how to cure these illnesses—this was the central contribution of the FCC in these situations (Nevins was not a member of the FCC, however). Nevins also said, "We are not promising to accomplish anything. We merely hope that a great number of people will be interested enough in the projected program to attend any, or many, of the meetings next week, in which they may be interested."[15] All too often this seemed to place the responsibility for work in the hands of local people. Obviously, if they believed local people already had the resources and the will to solve the problem, there hardly would have been a need to implement a clinic. Technically it was true that the clinic sought to diagnose problems and gather information about the local community, but the very purpose of these efforts was to provide concrete solutions to problems. It seems a case of willful ignorance to suggest that major social problems in a local community that required such outside experts and community leaders required or called for a mere diagnosis.

What these reports did provide were detailed analyses of the complex ways in which racism, oppression, and exclusion worked in many American communities. The Youngstown clinic revealed the severe housing shortage in the area and substandard housing in the poorer areas. As one report stated, "Field trips into the poorer districts have uncovered rather astounding facts and figures on the subject of sub-standard housing." One thousand "so-called homes" in the city were without any basic utilities such as lights, cooking appliances, or heating. One quarter of the city's dwellings were considered substandard. The report suggested various plans for meeting postwar housing demands.[16] Invariably, these reports highlighted the problems of the poor and oppressed, and gave detailed attention to issues of race and ethnicity, especially as the FCC ventured into western cities such as Portland, Oregon, and Los Angeles, where racial and ethnic minorities included Mexicans, Japanese Americans, Chinese Americans, and other ethnic groups. One should not trivialize the value of these reports, which were brought before various authorities in local municipalities. Much discussion ensued about the nature of these reports, which were often mentioned or summarized in local newspapers. This was a key part of the FCC's educational project in its broader race relations efforts.

Like many of its other race relations projects, the FCC's clinics brought whites, Blacks and other minority groups together to work on common problems. It was an interracial endeavor, but even more, it was a new tool to deal with an increasingly complex society of various minority groups making competing claims to citizenship and equal justice in American society. These clinics provided enormous amounts of data about the social, economic, and political conditions in local communities, and brought to light the many problems that various minorities faced, especially the difficult adjustments demanded by the war and the employment of minority groups in defense industries. These clinics were also an exemplification of the FCC's reliance on the social sciences to provide an accurate assessment of the hidden issues in a given community. Even so, Haynes and others felt that accurate knowledge alone was not sufficient. Action was required. The churches and communities were called upon to "practice brotherhood now," the Department's slogan by the 1940s. These clinical techniques were justified by their incorporation into a Christian theology of brotherhood, which was capacious enough not only to include the minority groups within a given community, but also to enlist labor, business, and leaders of other organizations to share in the common goal of community building and peaceful resolution of conflicts (Catholics and Jews were especially involved in workshops in midwestern cities). They were one of the many tools used to realize a theology of brotherhood.

Competing Theories of Personal and Social Change

Coming from different backgrounds and denominations, and often bringing in different speakers from other commissions or departments, it was inevitable that people in the Department of Race Relations would disagree about how best to implement changes in race relations. Sometimes debates emerged over what precisely was the nature of the race problem. Attempts to formulate plans for personal and social transformation rested on implicit and explicit assumptions and theories about anthropology (that is, the nature of human persons), the means of social change, how prejudicial attitudes are formed, and what kinds of oppositional practices would be necessary to bring about changes in society and within churches and individuals. The FCC also brought a peculiar dimension to the broader debate about social and political change. While organizations like the NAACP used techniques similar to those of the FCC and there was significant overlap in the kinds of issues they tackled, the FCC's internal documents indicate that leaders felt a special burden placed on their shoulders, because the organization represented churches. Churches were regarded as more than merely secular organizations. They were witnesses to the workings of the divine in history.

They were, ideally, representations of Christ's work of reconciliation. Yet, as one exasperated report of the Department put: "The Christian Church is in the dangerous and embarrassing situation where secular agencies often appear to take a higher and more consistent stand on a spiritual and ethical question than the Church itself."[17] Goading the churches to adopt or even recognize these various techniques of transformation—clinics, interracial contacts at Race Relations Sundays, anti-lynching campaigns—proved the most frustrating part of the FCC's work. This sense of frustration, and a heightened awareness of the tarnished reputation of Christian witness, were constant refrains in the Department's meetings. From its perspective, this transformation and witness was the unique responsibility and the peculiar burden of Christians in the world.

Discussion about the role of the church came up again and again in these meetings. How should the FCC relate to churches? What role did churches have in the world? What precisely was the FCC's role, and how should it motivate churches? From its inception, though it was clear that the FCC did not have authority over local churches and was not commissioned to affect church polity or statements of belief, its founding statement left open a wide arena. It was to "provide for a close and effective working together in order to secure larger combined influence for the Churches in matters affecting the religious and the moral and social condition of the people, so as to promote the application of the law of Christ in every relation of human life."[18] With such a broad mandate of applying the law of Christ (which was not clearly defined) to every relation of human life, there would inevitably emerge debates about its appropriate role and sphere.[19] Many of these discussions were about what churches should do about concrete issues such as lynching, economic inequality, and segregated housing. But attention to these concerns forced council members constantly to reflect on their theories of social change. After all, various ways of altering existing social structures were necessarily compared, and the FCC tried to square its suggested means with the "law of Christ" as they understood it.

On October 21, 1938, F. (Frederick) Ernest Johnson, a professor of education at Columbia University's Teachers College, delivered a talk on how to attack existing social problems and the best ways of accomplishing a change in prejudicial attitudes. Johnson, who was also a minister, was the executive secretary of the FCC's Department of Research and Education, and had formerly served on the Commission on the Church and Social Service. Johnson was a key figure in articulating a theory of social change. He had already published *The Church and Society* (1934), which was a forceful reassertion of a chastened social gospel that sought to come to terms with the harsh critiques of Christian liberalism by the likes of Reinhold Niebuhr, especially in his *Moral Man and Immoral Society* (1932). Johnson was regularly present at discussion and policy sessions of the Department of Race Relations. In his 1938 address, he advocated what he called a healthy separation of action and education. He told members of the department's gathered standing committees that they needed to adopt a new conception of education that gave some place to the importance of the past in developing tenacious habits of prejudice, and that recognized "that there are certain rigidities that cannot be broken through overnight." Johnson insisted that this respect for the past could be combined with dynamic and "explosive" elements of Christianity to foster positive changes in race relations. In talking about churches' efforts to end segregation from within, he stated: "In a community situation we have a powerful Negro vote that helps to swing things. We do not have that compulsion in the church. When the church breaks new ground in the social field we can say at least that it is voluntary; where frequently the community changes come about through compulsion and pressure."[20] The voluntary nature of churches, in contrast to growing legal pressures to change other organizations outside of the churches, would prove to be one of the most difficult obstacles to the FCC as it sought to influence churches through the only means available to it: moral suasion, by appealing to the divine origin of churches as (ideally) instruments of God's work in the world.

Johnson emphasized "intimate contacts" as crucial to Christianity, a "tremendously social religion." What he seemed to be saying was that, somehow, rich fellowship through voluntary means would have to be the way forward in the church. He insisted: "I do not think the Church will have a great power in the interracial field except as it comes to partake of fellowship of an interracial character. Our social pronouncements have been ineffectual, have run so far from what we are able to do within our fellowship. You are not going to be able to make a great impact on the community except as a result of a spiritual force from within."[21] Despite his brief comments about "explosive" elements in Christianity (which he did not elaborate on), Johnson recommended to the committee a "slow process of education through action." He concluded that the race problem in the South would not yield to a direct attack, thus implicitly suggesting an indirect approach.[22] Respondents to this talk seemed frustrated at its generalities, its seeming lack of concrete knowledge of real conditions on the ground in the South, and its elevated claims about Christian brotherhood when Blacks and whites remained separated in and outside of the churches. Those listening were apparently irked at Johnson's repeated comments about "rigidity" being a formidable barrier to Christian attacks on racial oppression, as if his suggestions rendered their tactics impotent or made the race problem insurmountable. Because they sounded like a critique of the department's (and, more generally, the FCC's) programs, Johnson's remarks about the inefficacy of pronouncements did not go over so well. Thus his claim noted above, "You are not going to be able to make a great impact on the community except as a result of a spiritual force from within," was received as an indictment of the FCC. But what could a bureaucratic entity like the FCC do to foster a "spiritual force" from within churches? And what precisely was this "spiritual force" and what relationship did it have to actual social change? Johnson's reference to "spiritual experience" must have discouraged some of those present, because the way he described it suggested that all "external efforts" by organizations like the FCC could only go so far if they did not coincide with such experience within individuals.

After Johnson concluded his speech, Mrs. Ida. L. Wallace, director of the Women's Church Activities Committee and a member of the African Methodist Episcopal Church, asked, "Isn't there something that feeds our spiritual self so that we do what we could not do through ourselves alone? Is there anything to that belief any more?" At this point, the discussion ended, leaving Wallace's pointed question hanging in the air. Though the notes in the FCC's internal memo indicate that a lunch session interrupted the meeting, perhaps those present were not sure how to respond to her query, or were irritated by its directness. It is not clear if Wallace directed her question to the standing committee or specifically to Johnson. Both were potential candidates for the critique embedded in her question. Directed to Johnson, it was a request for clarity: who or what sustains the spiritual self? What is the source of a "spiritual experience" and how does it empower Christians to do what they do not inherently have the strength to accomplish? After all, Johnson had painted a rather bleak picture of the efficacy of church work, and seemed to be so cautious about direct approaches to racial problems because of his belief that they would produce a backlash that he essentially offered a gradual and weak proposal for social change (which reacted limply to entrenched prejudices and customs). Wallace seemed to be hungering for a more robust source of spiritual strength and a clearer call for social engagement by a cadre of empowered Christians.

Wallace's question expressed a desire for a richer and more straightforward assertion of divine empowerment. Was she chastising the committee for granting too many deterministic constraints to the environment? Perhaps, but maybe she was also calling upon them to be more open about their Christian faith and what she felt God or the Holy Spirit could do to inject spiritual strength in believers to transform the world, despite the odds against them. Certainly she was frustrated with the minute analyses, the cautious suggestions, and the apparent concession that Christians ought merely to settle for outright racial oppression for many more years, while merely chipping away at the surface and attacking only its ugliest manifestations. This longing for a source of divine empowerment was a signal of dissatisfaction with certain elements of liberal Protestantism (in this case, expressed by an African American woman in the department).

Although too much can be made of one person's critique during a particularly lively meeting, evidence from other meetings suggests that at stake here was an aspect of liberal Protestantism that was identified by historian William G. McLoughlin. He argued that, in contrast to the "romantic evangelicalism" of the Second Great Awakening (with its emphasis on perfectionism, free will, and the miraculous), much of liberal Protestantism of the early twentieth century saw God's power as "locked into nature's laws" (what William Hutchison regarded as a liberal or modernist tendency to see God as immanent in human developments).[23] Based on this understanding of nature, humans were not free to leap over nature's laws or culture to challenge the often harsh realities of life. Liberal Protestantism was thus shorn of miraculous and transcendent qualities and, by extension, gave more emphasis to the shaping forces of culture and the environment.[24] McLoughlin concluded that, for all of its optimism about the inevitability of progress, liberal Protestantism was "fundamentally conservative." He was not necessarily speaking about the Social Gospel, which he regarded as a progressive minority wing of liberal Protestantism.[25] Though McLoughlin rightly noted that liberal Protestants tended to be cautious, and granted extraordinary power to culture and environment as shaping and constraining forces on the individual, it was precisely this emphasis on the social environment that liberated liberal Protestants (especially members of the FCC) from the older individualistic ethos that essentially blamed individuals for poverty, misfortune, and hardships in an urban environment that was dominated by industrial giants. The tenacity and strength of local cultures and traditional prejudices were indeed factors in the tentative and hesitant steps taken by leaders of the FCC, but it was this very focus on the broader social environment that incited their critique of the problems of urban industrialism and structural injustice.

The leaders of the FCC, in their struggle to come up with a forceful plan for social change, demonstrated the prescience of Walter Rauschenbusch's reflections. In his *Christianity and the Social Crisis* (1907), published just a year before the formation of the FCC, Rauschenbusch chided old-line evangelicals for their one-sided emphasis on personal morality and private conduct. He wrote that when they dealt with "public wrongs, they often exhibit a curious unfamiliarity with the forms which sin assumes there, and sometimes reverently bow before the devil's spider-webs, praising it as one of the mighty works of God."[26] Rauschenbusch was not favorably impressed with the captivating power of this new, industrialized urban environment, which he regarded as enslaving and thus hindering visions for social change. He argued for repentance for social sins, whereby Christians themselves acknowledged their complicity in the system and their blindness to its many evils, and "faith in the possibility of a new social order," which could serve as the foundation for social change. Without these two elements, a recognition of the tenacity and depth of social evil *and* hope in a new reality (the Kingdom of God), Rauschenbusch doubted that there would be a real possibility for social change.[27] The FCC alternated between these two poles, at times feeling impotent to effect social change because it was so taken with the intractable nature of racial oppression. At other times, the FCC summoned a vision of Christian brotherhood and unity, calling upon Christians to muster the resources of the Christian tradition to change the world. There was always a tension between a "reasonable" assessment of means to effect social change and an appeal to "emotional enthusiasm" and moral power to inspire and motivate Christians to alter the world.

In 1945, Haynes summarized what he saw as the appropriate function and strategy of churches in race relations. Their task was to replace "caste attitudes" and patterns by "fostering and applying the ideal that all human beings are members of the family of God, who has no favorites." The churches must regularly teach that every human being is of "inestimable value" and has an "equally inherent right of life, liberty and pursuit of life's satisfactions."[28] Churches generally went about instilling these truths through setting forth human values based on the ideal of the fatherhood of God and the brotherhood of man, and by developing social action and social service that would extend those values to everyday race relations. Haynes felt that the Department was already doing this through its various projects and that, so long as it aimed to change "personality attitudes" and "behavior patterns," it would be moving towards its ultimate goal of transforming people in local communities. He argued that the Department "aims to correct existing prejudiced attitudes and patterns, to prevent the growth of new ones, and to explore and foster advanced attitudes and patterns in church and community groups in harmony with the idea of the equality of all racial and cultural groups in the family of God."[29] This was Haynes's most succinct description of the means and ends of the Department of Race Relations. No language of coercion or struggle is evident in his grander vision. Changing attitudes and patterns. Making new persons and attacking unjust structures. While acutely aware of the nature of racial oppression, Haynes was generally optimistic about the strategy of combining interpersonal relations with efforts at structural change. This was also evidence of his strong commitment to a Christian theory of social change that was gradual and developmental.

Haynes's emphasis on interpersonal relations and cooperation was the guiding ethic of the Department, though it did not go unchallenged. In one session when members of different departments gathered in 1934 at a meeting of the committee on educational methods, Haynes's ideas were subjected to pointed critique. Haynes argued that a guiding philosophy should dictate the steps and means to achieve certain ends. For him, the church's role was to prevent and forestall conflict, "to prevent the fire before it starts." Mary Van Kleeck, one of those attending the meeting, challenged this emphasis on cooperation by arguing that sometimes a call for cooperative methods of social change amounted to no more than adherence to the status quo. Van Kleeck was actively involved in the YMCA, worked with the Russell Sage Foundation, and was an active member of the International Industrial Relations Institute, a social-economic planning body. She was deeply skeptical of capitalism and had just resigned in protest the year before from a federal advisory panel because she believed the New Deal refused to confront corporate domination. From this varied background, she was keenly attuned to the problems of labor and social change. Van Kleeck felt that cooperation was often no more than a "position which refuses to encourage struggle; it says we must have peace and cooperate." In her view, violence, or the fomenting of social conflict, was the only way forward.[30] She believed that the church should throw its weight behind various movements for social change, such as the labor movement. The guiding principle for her was certainly not cooperation. As Van Kleeck acerbically put it: "The churches should keep perfectly clear on the matter of social struggle and not let the question of unity and cooperation becloud our eyes." For her, human rights trumped property rights, and thus the church should always side with human rights if the two conflicted.[31] Probably her voice did not carry as much weight as Johnson's, given that she was not an active member of the Department of Race Relations. Parting ways with critics like Van Kleeck, Haynes rejected the notion that the church should foment conflict. His views generally prevailed in the Department, though in this particular meeting it appears that his arguments were subjected to criticism.

Repeatedly, debates about the role or function of the church emerged. More specifically, the question of the FCC's role as a "church agency" came up as well. At a 1932 meeting of a survey committee that studied the work of the Department, these issues were directly addressed when queries were raised about how churches should deal with economic justice. Should the FCC take a definite stance on labor issues? Should it favor workers over employers, siding with the labor movement more generally? F. Ernest Johnson argued that it was outside the scope of the FCC's function to educate black workers in ideas of collective bargaining. Haynes felt the issue was misstated and argued rather that the FCC was undertaking "labor education in labor problems" and using churches for that purpose. As he stated it: "The question is whether or not we should try to bring the ideal of justice to bear on race relations in economic life through the churches and in doing this whether we should seek to inform Negro churchmen of the labor problem involved in race contacts."[32] Thus he posed before those gathered the question of whether specifically it was the duty of the churches to "bring the ideal of justice to bear upon the problem disclosed in cotton-growing areas" (areas that were being surveyed and studied by the Department of Research and Education). Johnson was willing to concede that the FCC should educate its constituency and through that constituency the larger community, but he felt it should not single out any particular group. After much discussion, all seemed to agree that promoting justice in economic life was a part of the function of the Department, but disagreement emerged over how precisely to achieve this goal.[33]

Haynes argued that a whole philosophy guided the mission of the Department, and that it was this underlying philosophy that dictated the various means to a particular end. This claim did not sit well with some members. They held a more "pragmatic" view of means and ends, and of how the church should relate to the broader society. But for Haynes, ethical ideals and foundational Christian principles about social relations were essential as he sought (in the company of others) to formulate policy for the Department. His emphasis on cooperation, interpersonal relations, and interracial contact remained constant during his long career in the FCC. One clear example of Haynes's tendency to judge the results of the Department's implementation of a particular program by its underlying philosophy can be seen in a meeting that examined the efficacy of Race Relations Sunday (after it had been celebrated for almost a decade). Two significant questions were raised that had direct relevance to Race Relations Sunday: Is the basic social and psychological theory of race contacts underlying the technique of Race Relations Sunday observance scientifically sound? Is there danger that this type of work may be too much an end in itself and not lead to more constructive action? One member, Eva Hills Eastman, bluntly stated that she had no way of determining if Race Relations Sundays were successful. Haynes noted several "concrete cases showing results." He pointed to Akron, Ohio, "where outstanding individuals participated in preparing [a] mass meeting out of which grew fellowship of leading professional and business men" and pulpit exchanges, which were "significant because of [the] racial separation of churches." These examples given by Haynes were instances of what meetings were held, not what they accomplished in the broader community or what concrete results they produced. Haynes spoke as if the mere contact of Blacks and whites was a significant accomplishment and an end in itself, the very question raised by the meeting.[34]

Johnson responded to the first question by arguing that the Department's theory of race adjustment could be stated this way: racial groups come to know each other better and to appreciate each other more as they build up a basis of cooperation when they participate jointly in the solution of common problems. For him, this was a sounder basis for racial harmony than groups coming together to address problems of "race contacts" (an apparent jab at conferences to discuss "the race problem"). Haynes responded by invoking his foundational theory of "pleasurable" group contacts:

> The pain and pleasure experiences of large numbers of individuals of different racial groups that come in contact determine the emotional attitude or type of response of the groups as a whole. In the case of the white and Negro groups the masses of the two have been affected by the frictions and conflicts mainly outside of the churches and these in turn have determined the separation and attitudes of the racial groups inside the churches. Race Relations Sunday was started to provide mass contacts under circumstances where the experience would be pleasurable. The underlying idea is that the churches and other religious agencies should furnish such occasions for pleasurable contacts in contrast with the painful conflicts at other times.[35]

This is a remarkable example of Haynes's optimistic view of the power of interracial contacts and his sanguine take on the role of churches in developing newer attitudes and emotions. Nothing was said about the active role that southern churches played in developing and sanctioning a theology of separate races and their fierce opposition to miscegenation, on the grounds that it was against the divine order for purity of the races. To suggest that race relations within churches were "affected by the frictions and conflicts mainly outside" of them underplayed the active role of churches in creating and sustaining racial divisions. Of course, Haynes wanted churches to engage in interracial relations precisely so that attitudes and beliefs would be disrupted by concrete relations and practices. Even so, his theory seemed to reflect a rather naïve notion of the active role that churches were already playing in fostering division, as the Department's own complaints over the years had clearly indicated. Also, Haynes's concept of "pleasurable" contacts was always a bit hazy in terms of exactly what a "pleasurable" experience could accomplish in the broader society and in the disrupting of racial prejudices in individuals and churches. In the end, Haynes's theory of interracial contact was one grounded in his "whole philosophy," his sanguine view of human nature, and his ideal of cooperation and peaceful contacts. It rested fundamentally on his faith in the efficacy of his Christian philosophy of racial contacts. It was difficult, then, if not impossible, to prove that it was "scientifically sound," given that the philosophy incorporated its very means: interracial contacts are inherently good because of what they accomplish and because of the barriers they broke down. Who could disprove this, or what could prove that it was a sound philosophy? No clear answer emerged from the committee about whether these methods were "scientifically sound," except for Haynes's resolute belief that they were indeed sound and that interracial contacts would continue to be emphasized as central to the Department's mission. This emphasis on interracial contacts was its key mission to the churches and its part in helping them realize their role in the world.

5

Ecumenical Protestantism and the Limits of Racial Reform

In its annual report in 1925, the then-named Commission on the Church and Race Relations noted, regarding its Race Relations Sunday: "Of special significance for this year and for observance in 1926 is the broadening of the exercises to include relations of Jews and Christians, of whites and Indians, whites and Mexicans in the United States as well as of Negro and white Americans."[1] "Race relations" implied (as noted in chapter 1) a dynamism and fluidity that captured (for the commission) more accurately the nature of racial issues in the United States than the dehumanizing and static notion contained in the descriptor, "the negro Problem." Though protesting the injustices that Blacks suffered at the hands of whites, by choosing the label "race relations" the FCC sought to advance parity between races, rather than labeling racial problems strictly as a Black/white issue or implying that one race was superior to another. Then, too, the very expression meant that "relations" could change in the future and that they were fluid and ever evolving, and thus need not (and should not) remain in one place.

This nomenclature and its meaning had several functions in its historical context: 1) It sought to overthrow the dominant notion that one race was superior to another or that the problem of race in the US was to be attributed to the deficiencies of "the Negro," as the Negro problem label indicated. 2) It advanced a theory of race relations that was capacious enough to incorporate other minority or cultural groups beyond Blacks and whites. 3) It implied a dynamism about race relations that rejected the notion that Blacks were stuck in the foreseeable future in their social and economic situation, as white southerners often claimed, because their "racial character" hindered their advancement. 4) It suggested that relations (as Haynes articulated again and again) need not imply conflict or violence. “Relations” was in one sense a neutral term, but as used by Haynes and others, it connoted cooperation, peaceful encounter, and ultimately brotherhood between the races. To be sure, Haynes felt that much work must be done before relations between the races would become peaceful and on equal terms, but the name and concept implied progress and forward movement. In the very composition of the FCC’s Department of Race Relations, the organization would try to realize its ideal of peaceful and respectful cooperation between the races by staffing it with a significant number of African Americans, achieving almost an equal number of Blacks and whites in some of its committees. This ideal of interracial harmony was thus central to the mission of the FCC, but symbolism often took precedence over structural shifts both within the FCC’s leadership apparatus and its more general approach to social transformation. By looking in this chapter within the FCC’s own organization and concluding with its focus on broader interracialism, especially its addressing the issue of interracial marriage, we can see the limits of the FCC’s educational and gradual approach to racial reform.

Defining the Race Problem

After opening its eighth annual report on the challenges Mexicans were facing in the US, the notes of the department indicated: “The problems between white and Negro groups have continued to receive the main attention of the Commission because of their acuteness, because of the larger number of the two races involved, and because results achieved in this field will disclose principles and methods applicable to racial problems between other groups as the work of the churches at home and abroad may confront them.”[2] These continued explanations about where its emphasis lay in the annual reports (and in the internal documents of the Department) indicate that there was a need to explain and justify why race relations were addressed by most of its concrete programs in terms of the Black and white divide. The department’s attention to immigrants, Mexican Americans, Native Americans, and Asian Americans grew over time so that by the 1940s the department was not only debating how to frame the issue of race relations, but how to capture accurately its work in the very name of the department.

When the Department began its work in 1921, racial conditions were in a state of flux in the US. Millions of Blacks were now in northern and midwestern urban centers. Massive numbers of Jewish and Catholic immigrants from Southeastern Europe had settled in the cities over the past four decades, interrupted only by the War. Racial categories themselves were in a state of flux.[3] As noted in chapter 1, there emerged in the 1920s a lively debate among liberal thinkers and educators about the "cultural gifts" that immigrants and minority groups brought to the nation. This emphasis on gifts was a rejection of the melting pot theory, which asserted that immigrants and minority groups must conform to and assimilate into a white mainstream American culture, thus shedding their distinctive customs and ethnic particularities.[4] A "cultural pluralism" theory envisioned each distinctive group making its own contributions to the American nation. This cultural pluralism was often framed as a negative reaction to an increasingly hostile movement to Americanize the nation's immigrants to norms favored by an older white Protestant elite.[5] Though a Protestant organization, the FCC was one of the groups to advance a notion of "cultural gifts," especially by sponsoring the Harmon Awards for Black artists and by highlighting the contributions of Native Americans, Mexican Americans, and Asian Americans. It envisioned a multicultural democracy in incipient form when it extended this claim of cultural gifts to many minority groups, not just Blacks. The call for minority participation and sharing in the governance of the nation would become a more mature project by the 1940s.

There were several concrete ways in which the FCC demonstrated its commitment to addressing ethnic and minority concerns beyond the Black/white divide. George Edmund Haynes was the key figure in projects to display the cultural gifts and contributions of Black Americans. He especially highlighted "Negro contributions" in humor, drama, music, literature, art, and religion. With his comments about "cheerfulness of heart under hardship" and his grand generalizations about the "Negro soul" pulsating with rhythm and feeling "even when he walks and works," one finds an attachment to an older view of romantic racialism that was being promoted and challenged in the 1920s.[6] Yet Haynes's objective was to improve race relations by displaying Black talents. The Harmon Foundation Awards for Negro Distinguished Achievement was one such opportunity that Haynes created in his position at the FCC. The Harmon Foundation medals were awarded in eight categories: literature, music, fine arts, business and industry, science and innovation, education, religious service, and race relations. William Harmon agreed to provide $5000 annually for the awards and $3000 over a five-year trial period for administrative expenses. During its first years, from 1926 to 1930, Haynes served as the chief administrator of the awards.[7] Haynes wanted to show the world the hidden talents and gifts of Black people and thereby lessen prejudices against them. As such, Blacks could be seen as one among many of the nation's ethnic minorities who made their distinctive contribution to the national character.

Haynes believed that displaying Black artistic gifts was one among other "efforts to cultivate their unique powers and gifts to produce what other people may some day gladly receive."[8] Scholars have noted the immense importance of the Harmon Foundation in showcasing and legitimating Black visual art. It allowed African American artists to find a "distinct presence in the American art world" and contributed to the cultural flourishing of the Harlem Renaissance.[9] While not a theorist of art or literature, Haynes agreed with James Weldon Johnson, W. E. B. Du Bois, and other Black leaders who wanted to use art as a "strategic path toward racial advancement and the improvement of race relations."[10] He was instrumental in organizing these art shows and assumed the responsibility to publicize these events. Haynes selected the judges who chose finalists for the Harmon awards, and he himself presented the awards.[11] So eager was he to use these as venues to further his theory of interracial contacts and to manifest physically Black contributions that he sought venues and outlets so the exhibitions could be seen by Blacks and whites without discrimination. These art showings were sponsored by interracial and regional councils and they were featured in Black churches, libraries, public schools, and in local branches of the YMCA, some of the same channels that Haynes sought to disseminate the positive racial ideals of the FCC. The FCC sent out questionnaires to the different organizations that sponsored an art show "to provide statistics as to the number of white and Black visitors" and to gather information about the effect of these exhibitions on whites who saw them.[12]

Clearly, Haynes was more interested in Black art in sociological and educational terms than in its aesthetic value. The purpose of these events, in Haynes's race relations project, was to "educate the public about the achievements of American Blacks with the hope of improving race relations."[13] While this goal limited Black artists and carried different criteria of evaluation than artists and art critics, it was consistent with Haynes's theory of interracial contacts. It furthered his hopes of creating safe spaces and social environments where whites could behold and appreciate the contributions of Black Americans without the burden of a prejudicial "setting" shaping their judgment. Haynes apparently saw this engagement with Black art as a form of contact between the races, given his attention to the setting of these exhibitions. He also valued these engagements as moments to "teach" about race and the Black experience through visual portrayal and contact, rather than through blunt didactic or written discourse.[14] Haynes maintained an optimistic view that these cumulative experiences (alongside Race Relations Sundays and other projects of the FCC) would alter white prejudices and ultimately form new feelings and positive attitudes about Black people.

The FCC expanded its race work beyond the Black/white divide, and by the 1930s it emphasized the distinctive contributions of ethnic, religious, and immigrant groups to the nation. In 1929, the Department of Race Relations began publishing the Interracial News Letter in cooperation with the Social Service Committee of the Friends (Quaker) General Conference. Material in this newsletter reported on race as a worldwide problem, and included discussions of Mexicans, Indians, Blacks, and "Orientals" (Asian Americans).[15] As early as 1923, the Department had a full discussion about the "extension of the scope of the Commission's work to include the race relations of other types than white and Negro Americans." A Committee on Orientals was appointed. Similarly, the commission voted to cooperate with the Commission on International Justice and Goodwill on matters relating to Haiti, Africa, and race relations in other countries.[16]

The FCC's leadership in some of its committees followed the debates over immigration restriction in the 1920s. Whereas the 1921 and 1924 laws discriminated against southern and eastern European immigrants (through a quota system), the national origins formula enacted at the end of the 1920s had as its model the exclusionary measures previously adopted toward Chinese and Japanese immigrants, especially as codified in the Chinese Exclusion Act of 1882.[17] The FCC proposed a formal resolution against the Johnson-Reed Act of 1924, with its emphasis on national origins quotas, and as late as November 18, 1947, it called for removal of "the principle of discrimination in our immigration and naturalization laws respecting Orientals" and demanded that they might be eligible to become citizens.[18] Although these resolutions and the work of a number of individuals in the various departments of the FCC indicate that the organization was committed to a more capacious notion of nationhood than the dominant Anglo-Saxon paradigm, the undeveloped basis of the reasoning for the inclusion of Asian Americans (coupled with the common claim that their mistreatment in the United States would injure the reputation of missionary endeavors) does not suggest that this was a central concern or priority of the FCC's "race work" up to the 1940s. Even so, these concrete steps were small signals that race and ethnic concerns were broadening beyond its original formulation of the problem between the "two races."

Missionary concerns and the reputation of Christianity, especially among minority groups such as Black Americans, seemed to be the dominant themes in the FCC's early development of its program on race. After all, the commission began with the title of the Commission on Negro Churches and Race Relations (this name was changed rather quickly to the Commission on the Church and Race Relations). The specific catalyst for the commission's creation was a fear of race riots, and there was a desire to assist Black churches and deal more generally with racial problems in the entire country. Yet, over time, in addition to the reputation of Christianity and racial problems at home as an obstacle to missionary work, the FCC began thinking more deeply about the contributions of minority groups to American society and examining the nature of racial oppression and white supremacy. In other words, the "race problem" became more generally a concern about how to manage and foster cooperative "race relations" in a rapidly changing nation. But implicit from its inception, and made more explicit over the years, was the Department's theology of brotherhood, which in the American context meant interracial harmony among multiple racial groups enfolded within its ideal of cooperation and goodwill. This theology of brotherhood did not assume that racial conflicts would be solved easily and that mere interracial contact would ease prejudices, though Haynes was quite sanguine about the power of positive interracial contacts. In fact, through setbacks and obstacles, the FCC continued to hone its theology of brotherhood on race relations.

Embodying Racial Ideals

From the origin of the FCC in 1908, four major Black denominations—National Baptist Convention, Inc., African Methodist Episcopal, African Methodist Episcopal Zion, and the Colored Methodist Episcopal Church—were full members and remained so until 1950, when the FCC was folded into the National Council of Churches. The FCC sought to embody these same ideals of brotherhood when it formed the Department of Race Relations in 1921. Haynes, the Department's executive secretary, was to be one of the first African Americans who occupied a major leadership role in the FCC.[19]

Haynes shared the title of co-secretary of the Commission on Negro Churches and Race Relations (its title from its inception in 1921) with Will Alexander, a white southerner who was active in the leadership of the Council on Interracial Cooperation (throughout the 1920s and into the early 1930s, Katherine Gardner was also listed with the same title, co-secretary, as Haynes and Alexander). In 1948, Thomas Allen, a white man from Virginia, was elected co-secretary of the Department, working alongside J. Oscar Lee, an African American, who had replaced Haynes as executive secretary of the Department. This pairing of Black and white was apparently done as a model of what churches could accomplish in their midst.

The meetings of the Department were rather diverse for their time, in terms of racial and gender makeup. During its ninth annual meeting, of the sixteen members gathered, three are identifiably Black (based on their church affiliations and titles), and women made up nine of the total gathered (though this was not the total membership of the entire department, it is still notable because women also had a separate committee under the department, the Church Women's Committee).[20] With the exception of the NAACP, few private organizations achieved a rough parity of Blacks in their regular meetings and, in two instances, in high executive offices.[21]

The Church Women's Committee, which had organized in 1928, sponsored a number of interracial conferences of women, making extraordinary efforts to ensure that there was an equal number of Black and white women. After an interracial conference was held in Oberlin, Ohio in June 1930, Katherine Gardner was happy to report that there were fifty-four Black and fifty-five white registered delegates (with an additional sixty people from Oberlin and the surrounding area). These interracial conferences were held over several years; the delegates had frank discussions about the racial problems in the cities where they met and made attempts to "solve these problems in the light of Christian teachings."[22] These conferences had several purposes. They were forums for the discussion of interracial problems, with topics ranging from developing curricula to teach children and young people about how to practice "Christian race relations," to the economic hardships Blacks faced in a local community. Gardner also noted an additional function of these gatherings: "While the interracial conferences are planned as a means to an end through stimulating a desire for further action, they are also an end in themselves; for it is impossible for these groups of women to come together for several days of personal relationship without having a new conception of each other and a real revelation of the meaning of Christian fellowship."[23] In other words, though they began often with specific objectives in mind, the meetings of Black and white women (and later, in other contexts, Native Americans, Japanese Americans, etc.) became a social setting where, for the first time in many instances, Black and white women tried to relate to one another as fellow human beings and found mutual interests. Hence Gardner's emphasis on learning about the meaning of Christian fellowship in these settings, particularly in light of the fact that these women were often attending segregated churches on Sundays. These gatherings were some of the rare moments when interracial contacts occurred in a peaceful setting.

During these meetings and as a follow up in journals and magazine articles, Katherine Gardner urged the white participants to exert their influence to prevent discrimination against Blacks and to hire Blacks in their households. Many of these reports and discussions included lengthy analyses of the economic difficulties Blacks faced, and made suggestions about how women could ameliorate some of these harsh realities.

On December 17, 1931, the Church Women's Committee formed a subcommittee on hospitalization. The initial purpose was to see what could be done about the rank discrimination that Blacks faced in being turned away from hospitals (often in the face of critical illness), and in the refusal of hospitals to hire them. The subcommittee decided not to study the practices of hospitals in the northern and border states because of insufficient money, time, and expertise to produce an objective study. Nonetheless, great concern was expressed about lack of hospital facilities for Blacks, and the committee determined it "would undertake to secure a number of case stories showing discrimination against Negroes in hospital care, [and] in opportunities for training for doctors and nurses." They created a list of organizations that "are directly or indirectly affected by racial problems in health work." It was also noted: "One of the plans of this Committee is to make clear to the American public the widespread discrimination against Negroes in the matter of health facilities both for care and training."[24]

The efforts to study and change hospitals proved disappointing. Much of the work centered in New Jersey, in part because Gardner lived in and knew this area. Lack of funds and the refusal of hospitals to alter their policies toward Blacks were the most persistent obstacles. In February 1932, Gardner wrote with exasperation in the Federal Council's official bulletin about how difficult it was to change local practices. Hospitals would not admit Blacks, and would allow them to die rather than accept them for treatment. Gardner lamented: "Incredible as it may seem, when it comes to the color line, community mores are often so firmly fixed that even though a life hangs in the balance it does not occur to Christian men and women that there can be any departure from the established order." Yet, despite her frustration, Gardner still called upon "Christian forces" in America to end this discrimination against Blacks.[25] The actual results were just as dismal. By the end of 1935, the subcommittee (then called the Joint Committee on Nursing Opportunities working with the New Jersey Church Women's Committee) observed that, based on a survey of tax-supported hospitals in New Jersey regarding the employment of Black nurses, it was shown that no Black nurses were employed in the various hospitals. When this study was brought to their attention, several superintendents at the hospitals seemed interested in hiring Blacks, though two demonstrated personal prejudice or fear about hiring Blacks. The only concrete results after about eight years of study and efforts were reported in 1939, when two Black students were accepted in the training program at the Jersey City Medical Center. The committee was also looking into requirements for admission to nursing schools, and actively seeking qualified Black students to apply to these schools.[26]

These were instances when concrete actions were taken to deal with employment and health concerns. They had little result. Nevertheless, the ideals of the Department of Race Relations were being exhibited by the very fact of Black and white women engaging in cooperative efforts to confront the racial problems of their communities. Thus, in its internal makeup and in the activities and conferences that it sponsored, the FCC was seeking to embody the ideal of interracialism.

Yet one of the most common and frustrating obstacles was simply finding a meeting place for Blacks and whites. Most hotels in the Northeast and Midwest repeatedly refused to serve or house Blacks, compelling the FCC to acknowledge that segregation was not limited to the South. The meeting notes indicate a regular and urgent need to communicate in advance with hotels to avoid embarrassing or painful incidents, especially for Black delegates. So acute was the problem that the executive committee of the FCC adopted a formal resolution and action plan regarding hotel arrangements for interracial gatherings. It called for the elimination of all discriminatory restrictions against housing and serving Blacks in hotels, and stipulated that they must have free access to all rooms in hotels booked for the FCC's conferences.[27] Though the action plan was intended to provide clear guidelines for delegates who selected hotels for meetings, the major problem was how to implement the plan or find hotels that would agree to these stipulations (the FCC found that it often did not have the economic clout to compel hotels to agree to its stipulations). In the summer of 1934, the Department conducted a study on hotel options in the Midtown section of New York City, and found that only two hotels would even welcome "Negro guests."[28] This was a recurring problem throughout the 1930s and it was not limited to the FCC, given that every major hotel in New York City turned down hosting the annual dinner of the National Urban League because it required, among other things, an interracial dinner. Arrangements had to be made for the use of a ballroom and an outside caterer.[29] Clearly, the very implementation of interracialism could proceed in only a limited way so long as segregation was integral to the social structure of the nation.

While these efforts and the impact of these conferences were limited, their symbolic significance, their prescience in anticipating later developments in the social sciences, and their diagnoses of the nature of racism and racial oppression should not be slighted. When the Department sponsored the first National Interracial Conference—held in Cincinnati, Ohio, in 1925—it was setting a trend in promoting the latest research. Subsequent conferences dealt with topics such as "Race Problems in the Light of Social Research" (the title of the 1928 conference in St. Louis, Missouri). Many organizations sent representatives, including the National Urban League and the NAACP. The conferences' talks addressed segregation in the South, how children and adults learned prejudice, and the most recent findings that challenged scientific racism. The FCC was especially concerned with how to enlist and persuade churches to deal with racial problems; churches were not often examined in the social scientific literature. Time and again, the Department noted that churches were especially in need of sound social science, not just the Scripture and Christian teachings that they valued, as sources of authority on racial matters. While the FCC had a limited impact on the theology of segregation in southern churches and the de facto segregation of northern and midwestern churches, it made efforts to alter the patterns that bolstered and rationalized white supremacy and racial division within the churches. It found its distinctive niche in this arena.

The FCC was constantly trying to ascertain its unique role: how was it different from the NAACP, for example? What was distinctive about its approach? Its subject matter, the church, was one thing that made it unique. Another was its reiteration of a theology of brotherhood grounded in Christian teachings and the latest social science. This theology set it apart from most other religious organizations, even though there was clearly overlap in the issues addressed and in the assertion that democracy and Christian values were incompatible with racial oppression. Even so, as its critics claimed and its internal notes indicate, it was never clear that the FCC was all that distinctive in terms of how it sought to change racial attitudes and alter social customs. Its Christian teachings were certainly more explicit than those of the NAACP or the National Urban League, but these organizations were dealing with similar concerns. Its foundational theology, from its inception in 1908, sought to eliminate any distinction between the sacred and the secular.

Its formation of the Commission on the Negro Churches and Race Relations in 1921 (later renamed the Department of Race Relations) made it clear that lynching, disfranchisement, and segregation would be topics that the FCC could not avoid, especially if Black members and constituent denominations had any input, despite the department's continuing attempts to make a distinction between civic action and educational work to change attitudes and habit patterns (education being regarded as its principal task). Perhaps the worry and constant concern about what was distinctive about the FCC indicated that it was unsure what would remain unique about churches in the modern world. Perhaps also there was anxiety and uncertainty about how it ought to be different, in view of how "difference" often meant failure to address pressing problems that moderns could not fathom as outside the purview and reach of genuine humaneness and compassion, whatever the name or origin of the organizations that existed under circumstances of racial oppression in the United States during the FCC's four decades of existence. It would learn that "difference" was not always a good thing, and that God's work in the world proceeded through many channels, some outside of the churches (as its successor, the NCC, would articulate in its mature theology).[30]

Segregation Contrary to the Christian Gospel

Many factors motivated the FCC's eventual frontal assault on segregation: the difficulty in setting up interracial meetings, the struggle to find hotel accommodations, and its growing realization that the structural constraints of segregation limited interracialism. But in fact, even in the early 1920s the FCC's leaders were troubled about segregation, especially in churches. A maturation of its theology of brotherhood, and these practical constraints, combined to make the FCC, at its Columbus, Ohio, meeting in 1946, declare segregation to be against the fundamental tenets of the Christian gospel. As noted already, its theology of brotherhood challenged the very foundations of the South's theology of segregation, but specifically and directly articulating this attack on segregation and throwing its full weight against segregation in the churches and in the nation took some time. Nonetheless, it is worth noting that the FCC's statement against segregation came about nearly a decade before the Supreme Court's *Brown v. Board of Education* decision declared segregation in public schools unconstitutional. It was ahead of most similar-sized organizations in its attack on segregation and had consistently, from its origin, challenged segregated churches.

When reporting at the tenth annual meeting of the Department in 1931, Will Alexander noted what ten years had taught him and others in the field of race relations. He was struck by the "vast gulf" between leaders and the rank and file on how to solve race problems in churches. Alexander also stated that the basic problem was segregation, and although he did not suggest any grand gesture in response, it was quite a frank admission by a native southerner.[31] Complaints about the constraints and indignities imposed by segregation were repeatedly noted by those working in the field as they reported back to the Department. And this was not limited to the South, as was learned when plans were made to set up interracial clinics in midwestern cities or attempts were made to book hotels in northeastern cities. Segregation made interracialism attenuated and episodic at best.

A study by Department experts in 1932 called for plans to attack segregation "both within and without the churches and religious bodies." This was formulated alongside plans for civic justice and "a comprehensive program to foster justice in race relations in economic life."[32] There is no indication that the Department's leaders wrestled seriously with the incongruity of seeking civic and economic justice in race relations in a segregated society that denied basic human rights to Blacks. Even so, the call for desegregated churches was announced alongside a demand for radical alterations in civic and economic life. Whatever their intentions at the time, the Department's evolving theology of brotherhood and its attempts to bring about concrete improvements in race relations became incompatible with a system of legal segregation. It was only a matter of time before this incongruity was directly confronted.

In a confidential memorandum approved in 1942 at Riverside Church in New York City, the Department of Race Relations emphatically stated: "Because segregated churches are at variance with basic Christian and democratic principles their elimination should be the goal and steps should be taken immediately toward it."[33] It called on the churches "in the name of Christ" to contribute to interracial brotherhood and recognize that segregation was contrary to their "ecumenical character." By November 1945, the notes of the annual meeting indicate that a more comprehensive stance against segregation was being advanced. Segregation was labeled a "basic evil in human relations" and churches were called upon to regard it as their moral duty to end the practice. It was also stated: "the full influence of the Church should be exerted to remove all legal protection for or requirement of segregation, whether in the form of 'Jim Crow' laws, restrictive covenants in land titles or in any other form. We hold it to be ethically wrong to protect or require segregation by legal enactment."[34] Here was a direct attack on the system of segregation that existed in the entire nation, and a demand that the churches should actively seek to end it. This was the final formulation of the FCC's position before its official Columbus statement the following year.

At the special meeting held in Columbus, Ohio, from March 5 to 7, 1946, at which President Harry S Truman spoke about brotherhood, the FCC approved an official statement on "The Church and Race Relations." This document became the guiding light for its approach to segregation and racial discrimination for the remainder of the FCC's existence.

The significance of this statement has been lost, because most people today are not aware of the cultural authority that the FCC had at this moment—Truman was the second president to address one of its major gatherings. The Columbus document, first of all, regarded segregation as a national and not simply a southern or regional problem, noting that segregation is "accepted, with some differences of emphasis, in all sections of the country."[35] Rejecting the "separate but equal" doctrine, the statement argued that segregation "has always meant inferior services to the minority segregated" and that the system has never secured equal rights or facilities for Blacks because segregation is "always discriminatory."[36] Following from this view of segregation, the document stated that segregation was a concrete expression of the "inferiority-superiority pattern of opinions about race held tenaciously by vast numbers of Americans" and that this system, by its very oppression of minorities, imparted the notion to children and future generations that minorities were inferior. The statement was a direct refutation of the majority opinion in *Plessy v. Ferguson* (1896), which asserted that enforced segregation did not stamp a "badge of inferiority" on Blacks.[37] The Columbus document asserted that segregation was inherently discriminatory, necessarily treated Blacks as inferior to whites, and subjected Blacks to "constant humiliation" and "spiritual and psychological handicaps."[38]

Though all forms of segregation were rejected, whether enforced by law in the South, or by custom and tradition throughout the nation, the thrust of the document indicted segregation as antithetical to true Christian fellowship and unity in the body of Christ. Churches then were called upon to recover the "transformative power" of the early Christian community and "apply that power to the massive problem presented by race tensions in community life."[39] Churches were charged with getting rid of segregation within their own communions and examining the ways in which segregation and racial discrimination had affected or permeated their membership, worship services, employment practices, and fellowship opportunities. As the statement urged: "In order that the Church may remove the validity of the charge which the world makes when it says, 'Physician, heal thyself,' we urge our constituent members to correct their own practice of segregation" and formulate a plan of action to rid themselves of all forms of racial separation.[40]

The Columbus statement represented the maturation of the FCC's theology of brotherhood. It indicted segregation as unchristian in its character and a "violation of the Gospel of love and human brotherhood." In renouncing this system, the document urged churches to "work for a non-segregated Church and a non-segregated society." The early church was pointed to as embodying a "mysterious power in the unity of Christ's disciples" and molded by the "internal bonds of brotherhood."[41] This emphasis on the early Christian community was intended to incite churches to recover brotherhood, racial unity, and cooperative interracial fellowship as integral to Christian living and witness. As this developed theology indicated, the sincere desire of some Christians to have interracial fellowship would always be frustrated and defeated in a racially segregated society. Undoubtedly, this had been learned from the pervasive violence that enforced the segregation of Blacks in the South, but also from slights and humiliations that Blacks suffered in the FCC's attempts to organize interracial gatherings in midwestern cities and in northeastern hotels. The FCC argued that only an amelioration of racial tensions was possible, not true interracialism and "mutual helpfulness," so long as segregation remained.[42] This interracialism, while clearly with Blacks and whites primarily in view, also extended to "other minority groups," and the hope was that Christians would accept "all racial groups into the same religious society on the basis of equality."[43] Thus the Columbus document envisioned a multicultural church and a diverse society that included all ethnic and cultural groups. It was the FCC's fullest critique of racism and its clearest statement of the problem of race.

External and Internal Constraints

From 1946 to 1950, the last four years of its existence (and before civil rights activism would experience a significant shift in intensity), the FCC's Department of Race Relations (and the Federal Council as an entire institution) became involved in all the major race-related issues of the day: speaking out against segregation in the South, endorsing and providing commentary on President's Truman's Committee on Civil Rights, contributing to discussions of human rights at the United Nations, and providing an amicus brief on *Sweatt v. Painter*, the first in a series of cases that would eventuate in the *Brown* decision of 1954. At this point, the FCC was the most visible Protestant body taking a range of controversial stances on cultural, social and political issues. As David Hollinger has noted, leaders of the FCC were the public face of Protestantism during the 1940s.[44]

Yet, as prominent as the FCC was, there were indications of weaknesses within its ecumenical vision and shortcomings in its techniques to eradicate racism even before it was surpassed in cultural and political influence by the rising neo-evangelical movement, which had formed the National Association of Evangelicals (NAE) in 1942. Though what follows is by no means an exhaustive list of the FCC's shortcomings, this is an examination of the internal and external constraints faced by the FCC, focusing especially, though not exclusively, on its last few years of existence.[45] The point here is not that a decline in the influence of ecumenical Christianity was a foregone conclusion, though some of the issues raised do seem to have hinted at the decreasing fortunes of ecumenical Christianity in later decades. Specifically, the FCC's constant budgetary problems (churches contributed only limited amounts to its racial projects), its failure to reach and its rebuffs at the hands of the laity in many churches, its cooperative model and sometimes timid steps on controversial issues in racial reform, and its internal structural limitations (as a bureaucratic institution with highly educated and mostly white male leaders) were all factors in its diminishing influence and missed opportunities. It never had the support of most lay members of Protestant denominations, and it was the active opposition of evangelical leaders and their creation of alternative institutions that led to and coincided with its decline. This chapter then details a crucial historical moment when internal and external forces brought about the eclipse of the symbolic position that liberal Protestants held in American society, represented most notably in the FCC's conflicted position on race relations.

The Church Divide

The funding of the Department of Race Relations indicates that it was not as highly regarded by laity or denominations as other departments or commissions. That it was funded regularly by an annual grant of $5000 by the Russell Sage Foundation meant that it relied on this consistent source of income without having to vie for funds with other departments. This grant was given yearly from 1922 to 1943, decreasing to $2000 per year from 1943 to 1947. The FCC's executive committee passed a formal resolution in 1947, recognizing this steady source of assistance.[46] It is likely that without the philanthropy of the Sage foundation the Department would have been even more underfunded. Would the FCC have made up for these funds from other places? We cannot be sure, but what is certain is that churches and denominations were much more comfortable giving money for evangelism and international missions than for controversial projects like racial reform. This required the FCC to look beyond churches, often to philanthropic organizations and various donors to help fund its more controversial projects. This may also suggest why the FCC, apart from its detailed studies of local communities, often lacked contact with lay voices, especially conservative ones, about their feelings on race. It is doubtful, however, that it would have taken its more "prophetic" stance on race relations if it had heeded those voices.

When William Adams Brown, chairman of the Department of Research and Education, spoke in 1934 about the "Church and State in

Contemporary America," he noted a problem that Will Alexander, co-secretary of the Department of Race Relations, had also identified in 1931 in his assessment of his own department's work. Brown commented on the "existence of a dangerous rift between the views of the clergy of our churches and many of their laymen."[47] It is quite interesting (and rather unexpected) that Brown raised the issue of a separation between clergy and laity. The speech was really an eloquent statement of the FCC's philosophy of the church's role in the broader society. As members of the Department of Race Relations had done for many years, Brown argued that "the chief function of the church in its relation to the state must be one of education, or, in other words, of creating those attitudes and opinions which will make the Christian attitude toward life prevail over such wide areas as to make its application to specific social situations possible."[48] He acknowledged that though there was general agreement about the goal to be achieved, there was widespread disagreement about the means. No doubt it was here that the laity's and the clergy's views differed most profoundly, though one wonders if even the envisioning of specific goals was widely shared in the churches.

In its efforts to fight racism, the FCC quickly discovered that the closer it got to the ground, among local churches and in the thick of their issues, the less it could assume that people shared its Christian vision. It was clear that lynching was not regarded as a stain on the nation's character by all local church members who were, in many instances, untroubled about the violence against Black Americans. The FCC, of course, was not responsible for the intransigence and prejudices of local communities. Yet these factors do suggest that the FCC's emphasis on education and cooperation had significant limitations. For all Haynes's hopes for bringing Blacks and whites together, and despite all the talk about the educational function of the church, what was the use of pamphlets and information in those contexts where the primary contact between Blacks and whites was violent? These were the settings like Salisbury, Maryland, where grisly lynchings occurred and no sympathy was publicly expressed for the victims. Then there were the places where competition for jobs led to mutual suspicion, if not outright violence. Stressing a cooperative ideal could do almost nothing in such settings. The call to live up to a Christian ideal of brotherhood was a failure to acknowledge this violent reality.

Some of the FCC's reports on lynchings and economic disparities between Black and white farmers in the South noted ways that local churches contributed to the denigration of Blacks, and the FCC used the details in these reports to shame churches. To make them live up to their Christian vision by calling them out on their moral failings. One tactic was to alert churches to the obstacles they would face in missionary work abroad (among non-white peoples) if they continued to mistreat Blacks in the US. But there is little indication that the leaders of the FCC, even in the Department of Race Relations, recognized the extent to which churches, especially in the South, were active creators of racial distinctions and the way that evangelical culture in the South contributed to violence. Recent scholarship has explored the connections between piety, purity, and lynching in the South. It has argued that segregation was a religion, that the distinctions between good and evil in terms of white and Black skin were ways of establishing powerful religious moods and motivations. Black bodies became a part of the profane in this rendering of religious symbols. This religious culture did not simply sanction violence against Blacks, according to this interpretation, but rather it created Blackness as part of the profane world.[49]

Lynch mobs often saw themselves as instruments of divine wrath and retribution, protecting the sacredness of "white womanhood" from Blacks as "demonic" transgressors of the laws of racial purity. As Amy Wood writes, "These rituals did more than simply punish the Black 'demon' in their midst. Through their spectacular excess, they constructed a symbolic representation of white spiritual and moral superiority. Lynching rituals produced, in very stark and dramatic terms, dichotomies between Black and white as damned and saved, sinner and saint, which came to define white supremacy."[50] The FCC's language of Christian hypocrisy, while a critique of the practice of southern religion, did not account for this view of the connection between violence and religion. One exception may be found in 1931, when the FCC's Race Relations Department hired Rev. Howard S. Anderson, minister of the Williston, North Dakota, Congregational church, to conduct the investigation of a lynching in that area. Anderson made reference to a spirit of vigilantism and frontier justice as partial explanations of the lynching. He also noted that revival meetings were being held in Waterford, North Dakota, at the time the lynching took place. Anderson suggested "that the preaching of Old Testament ideas of retributive justice, which is usual in the region, may have had some influence in the matter."[51] In general, however, no attention was paid to religion's role in creating violent moods and motivation. Perhaps this view of religion was not imaginable for leaders of the FCC, who generally had a more optimistic conception of religion. In fairness, it is not clear what difference, if any, this interpretation of religion would have made, but it could have moved the FCC's critique of various churches beyond the language of hypocrisy. It might have moved them to address how violence was intertwined in religious practices in certain local cultures.

If differences existed between educated clergy and local church members on issues of life and death, then surely the FCC should have been more aware that differences probably existed in other areas. But the issue of lynching is complicated because the FCC really did make an effort to understand its causes. No doubt more could have been done to study not simply the conditions producing a particular lynching, but also the theology of local churches and members' views of the event. In many instances, however, ignorance (on the part of local people or the FCC) was not the problem. Many pastors and lay people simply rejected the FCC's ecumenical vision and its claim that lynching was a form of vengeful barbarism that had no place in a Christian society. On this issue, local pastors often shared the views of their constituents. Thus, the clergy-laity divide has to be specified in terms of place and context. In some instances, distance from the laity was not a case of elitism, but rather an independent stance on a morally troubling issue. From the

FCC's perspective, it was witnessing to a vital Christian truth and therefore had to stand apart from the laity. It was exercising its prophetic role of speaking the truth in love, even if it alienated itself from its constituents and the laity. That was the price it had to pay to be faithful to its identity and its calling.

The Limits of Brotherly Love

I have argued that, since its first eloquent articulation in the 1920s, the FCC's theology of brotherhood fundamentally challenged the theology of segregation dominant in southern churches and that was the effective practice of many northern and midwestern churches. While the theology of separate races justified the legalized segregation of Blacks and whites in the South, it was particularly directed toward the most intimate of relations: sex and marriage. When Gunnar Myrdal, the Swedish economist who studied the race problem in the United States in the late 1930s and early 1940s, reflected on the nature of racial issues, especially in the South, he concluded that prohibitions against marriage stood out most prominently. Myrdal felt that in its most concise meaning, the expression "no social equality" meant no racial amalgamation and preserving "the purity of the white race." The repugnance to and visceral revulsion against "intermarriage" was akin to "true taboos" and the notion of "not to be touched" in primitive religions, Myrdal asserted. The most straightforward and popular critique of social equality was posed in the form of a question: "Would you like to have your daughter marry a Negro?" Miscegenation, then, was seen as a fundamental threat to racial integrity and a segregated southern society.[52]

Myrdal noted that a whole system developed that upheld this order, with each plank having a relative significance as a protection against racial amalgamation:

A ban on intermarriage and other sexual relations between white women and Black men. This measure took precedence over all else. Other restrictions bolstered this primary taboo.

Various taboos and forms of etiquette in personal contacts: no meals together; Blacks could not initiate handshakes; they were denied entry through front doors of white homes; Blacks had to avert their eyes when approaching white women in public settings, etc.
Segregation in schools and churches, because such close contact could lead to forms of intimacy and approach social equality.
Segregation in hotels, restaurants, theaters, and other public places where people met socially.
Segregation in public transportation.
Discrimination in public services.
Inequality in politics, justice, and breadwinning and relief.

I have listed the various levels of segregation to indicate how segregation was viewed and interpreted by an astute observer who had spent years studying it. Modern scholarship indicates that a Protestant theology of segregation was crucial to legal arguments for anti-miscegenation statutes.[53] Because God had created the races as distinct and separate, it would violate the divine will to permit interracial marriage. As historian Jane Dailey has argued, "It was through sex that racial segregation in the South moved from being a local social practice to a part of the divine plan for the world."[54] This topic evoked such passionate feelings that even the NAACP tried to avoid it when crafting its strategy against various aspects of segregation, such as discrimination in higher education and restrictions against voting in the 1940s.[55]

Prior to its publication of the Columbus statement against segregation, the FCC had made little public comment directly about interracial marriage. Its theology of brotherhood, in my view, implicitly challenged all of the traditional arguments against the practice. Yet no comment on interracial marriage was included in the final Columbus statement. In the original draft, there was an entire paragraph on "Racial Segregation and Inter-Marriage." The draft was hardly a positive endorsement of interracial marriage. If anything, it was an attempt to quell fears about the possibility of widespread intermarriage in the event that legal restrictions were repealed. The key positive assertion was that in a "democratic and Christian society such as we dream of in America, there can be no legal limitation, based on race, creed, or national origin alone, upon free relationships among people."[56] In articulating its rather dubious claim that interracial marriages would be rare if different groups were "thrown together on terms of equality," the draft asserted that "each race is rightfully grateful for its own heritage and desirous of preserving its own identity." With a remarkably condescending and paternalistic tone, the draft continued: "What each race chiefly desires and needs is not so much the opportunity for intermarriage as the recognition of its equal dignity with other races within the family of mankind." Nonetheless, it concluded that "the fear of inter-marriage cannot be allowed by the Christian Church to perpetuate the segregation pattern" and that the "presence and variety of racial groups within the American community is to be accepted gladly and reverently as full of possibilities under God's purpose for the enrichment of life."[57]

Even this weak "endorsement" of the possibility of interracial marriage did not appear in the final draft of the Columbus document. Nor did support for interracial marriage appear as a "personal" or "social" right in the FCC's 1948 statement on "The Churches and Human Rights."[58] The interracial marriage paragraph in the Columbus document was simply marked "eliminate" in the internal files of the FCC. No explanation was given for its removal. Historian Barbara Savage argues that Benjamin Mays and others had proposed even stronger language, but that the fear of intermarriage among council members prevented even this mild statement from being included. For Savage, this was another example that even liberal Protestants were unwilling to confront the question of interracial marriage, even when goaded and prompted by leading African Americans.[59] One can only speculate about the precise reasons why the FCC did not formally endorse or even discuss interracial marriage in the Columbus document. It had taken a public stand on a number of issues, offering resolutions against restrictive covenants and forcefully repudiating segregation. Fear is a possible cause, but the FCC had indeed taken a number of unpopular stances. Its philosophy of interracialism and its practice of interracial and mixed meetings had been in existence for several decades. Expediency and wariness about a highly controversial issue seem the likely explanations for this failure to address interracial marriage. Though the FCC's stance was troubling and indicated a limit to its theology of brotherhood, it should be noted that even the NAACP avoided mention of interracial marriage or sexual relations between Blacks and whites throughout the 1940s and into the 1950s, when it endorsed the series of decisions that culminated in the *Brown* decision. This topic was seen as too hot to handle. It was nearly a decade and a half before the Supreme Court, in *Loving v. the Commonwealth of Virginia* (1967), declared unconstitutional the various anti-miscegenation statutes in the United States.[60] Even so, this grand opportunity for the FCC to speak forcefully was lost, and instead fear, expediency, and a weak and faltering witness to true interracialism prevailed.

The Moral Power of Religious Motivation

When George Haynes summarized the work of the FCC in a confidential memorandum in 1932, the first item on the list was the FCC's crusade against lynching, because it was a life-and-death issue. Haynes also noted the promotion of interracial conferences, attempts to bring about justice in the realm of economic life, the work of the women's committee, the organization of state and local groups, a massive project of publications on race, and sponsorship of the Harmon Awards (which recognized and promoted Black artists), among other things. Haynes divided these various activities into four fields: civic justice, building attitudes and habit patterns, economic justice, and appreciation of Black achievement.[61]

In Haynes's mind, the appreciation of Black achievement and the changing of racial attitudes were linked in important ways. In this memorandum, he captured how the FCC attempted to balance its internal emphasis on promoting interpersonal relationships and attitudinal change with its attention to broader societal problems. In reflecting on this approach to addressing these problems, Haynes wrote that they had tried to "unite social engineering based upon careful scientific research and survey with the emotional enthusiasm and moral power of religious motivation" to achieve their objectives.[62] Though this was a description of the techniques and tools of the FCC, in practice it also meant that its various projects would include partners, especially in procuring and utilizing "careful scientific research." For example, experts, sociologists, political scientists, and church bureaucrats were recruited to study lynching, because of the need for authoritative research to convince Congress to address it, but also because of the unwillingness or inability of pastors and clergy to handle such issues. But the internal dynamics of the FCC indicate that it was an ecumenical strand of Christianity that wedded theological education with social scientific research in almost all of its projects. This was in part a new trend in which social science served as a handmaiden to theology, to supplement and make concrete its application and relevance to the modern world.[63] The appeal to "emotional enthusiasm" and "moral power" reflected an awareness of the powerful force of religious commitment, and skepticism about relying solely on "science" or a secular basis for social reform to elicit the necessary will to carry it through. On this point, David Chappell may have been right about secular liberals needing stronger conviction and greater power to do something about segregation in the South, but Haynes's reflections indicate that the FCC does not fit into the trajectory that Chappell narrates.[64] Haynes found compelling reasons to wed social science and Christian faith; he also utilized sources and motifs for suffering and sacrifice from the Christian tradition to incite Christians to action in the face of hardship.

As inheritors of a rich tradition, in which suffering and persecution were the lot of Christians in a hostile world and appeals to divine power were common, the FCC drew upon these traditions for strength to move forward. Prayers at the beginning of Department meetings, penitential prayers for divine judgment against lynchers and for spiritual sustenance for Christians who challenged the system of white supremacy, scriptural references to divine action and to Christian empowerment in the world, and testimonies of the church's work in the world at present and in history were all part of the "spiritual cosmos" of the FCC.[65] Though "social engineering" should perhaps be better rendered "social reform," given the piecemeal nature of the FCC's project and its less-than-radical call for changing the nation, religious motivation and enthusiasm was a crucial element in its efforts at social transformation. It is this emphasis on religious motivation that I have highlighted in this work, pointing to the power of religious conviction as a source of progressive social change. This narrative is also an attempt at historical retrieval of a strand of Christian thought and practice that has not fared so well, in recent scholarship, and has been obscured or overlooked because much scholarly work has been so preoccupied with the Christian Right and its approach to political and social reform. Retrieval, then, is necessary. As historian Jill Gill writes, the FCC was formed from a "desire that Christians should rediscover their inherent God-given unity with one another as the living 'body of Christ' in the world."[66] The application of that ideal of unity in the church to racial reform and the unfolding of their theology of brotherhood have been the central concerns of this narrative.

Conclusion

Legacies of Liberal Protestantism and Race

Historian James Findlay argues, in his excellent book on race relations and the National Council of Churches (the successor to the FCC), that it was in 1963 that this organization and the mainline Protestant churches became supporters of direct action in African Americans' struggle for racial justice.[1] Conferences, studies, radio broadcasts, and information-filled pamphlets had represented the FCC's dominant approach to race relations up to 1950. These were not street folk. They had hoped to change attitudes, appeal to ideals to shame the nation to change its ways, produce mountains of evidence to disprove dominant theories of Black racial inferiority, and bring people together to experience and express mutual appreciation and goodwill for their distinctive contributions as part of the diversity of God's created order. Yet there was a longing for something more. George Haynes once expressed this in his claim that he had hoped to evoke and utilize the "emotional enthusiasm" and moral power of religion to bring about change. But none of those techniques to realize this vision of racial justice involved direct action, but rather more conferences by a diverse array of groups: Catholics, Jewish organizations, secular institutions devoted to single issues, and local politicians. The conference and papers remained the dominant modes. Preaching or public speaking to appeal to an audience continued in church contexts. The FCC disseminated pamphlets to multiple constituents, but putting bodies in the streets and engaging in actions that could have brought businesses to a halt or altered the ebb and flow of life in a local community were actions beyond the purview of the FCC's model of social change. Perhaps its area of greatest impact was its ideological challenge, in its theology of brotherhood that ultimately gained ascendancy with the emerging Civil Rights movement and eventually became associated with "true Christianity" in its normative view of race relations.[2]

Given its bureaucracy and the often staunch opposition from member churches, it would have been inconceivable that the FCC would have supported direct action of any kind in the South before 1950—merely conducting a serious and impartial study of lynching became the subject of controversy, and led to the author of the study being ridiculed and ostracized in southern communities Then, too, the threat of physical harassment and violence was always present. We have seen the fate of Broadus Mitchell, even in the state of Maryland, for his analysis of lynching. Apart from these concrete challenges to social mores, the very theology of brotherhood was associated (in white southern Protestant Christianity) with integration—a violation of the divine separation of the races, a Christian fantasy that imagined no "natural boundaries" between the races, and an illusory peace and harmony before the cataclysmic, world-upending return of Jesus. In 1954, James F. Burks, pastor of Bayview Baptist Church in Norfolk, Virginia, preached that the "idea of the 'universal fatherhood of God and brotherhood of man' is man's concoction and contradicts the word of God."[3] Burks attacked the National Council of Churches and "liberal clergymen" for their "tactics and brainwashings" and specifically called for segregation of the races and rejected the *Brown* decision and any theological position that promoted brotherhood and integration. This rejection of a theology of brotherhood indicated that, by the 1950s, segregationists were on the defensive and the NCC was no longer a lone voice, especially since *Brown* made the religious defense of segregation more urgent.

Theological reflection and a particular form of social thought were also factors in the FCC's gradualist approach to racial reform. As an internal critic of religious and political liberalism, Reinhold Niebuhr wrote: "All social co-operation on a larger scale than the most intimate social group requires a measure of coercion. While no state can maintain its unity purely by coercion neither can it preserve itself without coercion."[4] This emphasis on coercion as necessary to social change is what set Niebuhr apart from liberals of the kind that associated with or were a part of the FCC. They repeatedly invoked goodwill and pleasurable experiences between individuals and groups as the way forward. In one of her widely disseminated works on racial and cultural issues, Rachel DuBois argued that the "fundamental problem of our own land and of the world today is this problem of personal relationships." Having worked in the FCC's Women's Department and offering a view similar to many in the Department of Race Relations, DuBois believed that progress in the cultural and racial realm could not be "achieved by any kind of coercion, mental or physical, but by learning to care for one another's welfare."[5] These quite different theories encapsulate the salient aspects of this debate on social change. They shed light on Findlay's critique of the FCC's educational aims, and the break from its approach (similar to the break from the NAACP) that occurred with the nascent Black freedom struggle of the 1950s. Friendliness, harmony, and mutual cooperation were the buzzwords of the Department of Race Relations for its nearly three-decade tenure. Christian nonviolence, personal and professional decorum, a certain timidity, and confidence in a gradualist approach to personal and social transformation only chipped away at rather than frontally assaulted systematic racial oppression.[6] And yet the significance of the ideological battle for church members' attachment to received interpretations of Scripture and critiques of the dominant scientific racism of the time must not be trivialized, even as we acknowledge these glaring shortcomings of the FCC in hindsight.

Recent scholarship indicates the enduring explanatory power of segregationist theology for white southerners during and after the Civil Rights movement. As J. Russell Hawkins writes, "such theology fueled southern white Christians' defense of Jim Crow segregation in their society and churches. Drawn from a particular bible reading, segregationist theology became the lifeblood of a segregationist Christianity around which many white southerners ordered their lives. . . ."[7] The FCC was waging the struggle over biblical interpretation and divine sanction for decades before the emergence of Civil Rights activism. The FCC's persistent claims about brotherhood and human kinship "kindled rebellion among religious defenders of racial hierarchy and separation."[8] What these white southerners feared was an alternative theological basis for human relationships—especially an ecumenical Protestant theology of brotherhood that challenged its reading of Scripture, appealed to divine authority, and claimed that racism and racial separation were heresies introduced into the Christian churches as a result of slavery and European colonization. This theological vision impugned the whole system of segregation in the South. Hence the repeated instances of white southerners (and northern white conservatives) labeling organizations such as the FCC (and later the NCC) as elitist, outsider, misguided, Communist-influenced or infiltrated, and thus anti-biblical or "unscriptural" in their support of integration. Having the moral high ground in the ideological and theological battle mattered to these Christian defenders of segregation who appealed to Scripture and Christian orthodoxy to authorize and naturalize their racial views.[9] The theology of brotherhood was a direct threat to their longstanding theological edifice. What James Findlay writes about key theological texts sponsored by the NCC in the 1960s is also true of the FCC's Department of Race Relations prior to 1950: its writings, publications, workshops, Race Relations Sundays, and teachings "challenged thousands of lay people and clergy to think in new ways about the church's position in the world. . . ."[10] Its theology of brotherhood was its most significant contribution to race relations, though it did make notable anti-lynching efforts and provide forums for face-to-face workshops, limited interracial church gatherings, and public conferences. The theological argument for a more capacious human kinship was its most enduring ideological contribution that would eventually gain ascendancy during and after the Black freedom struggle, all hard-fought historical achievements against a powerful countervailing theological tradition and centuries of racial oppression.

ACKNOWLEDGMENTS

I have been working on this book for over a decade now. I spent more time at the Presbyterian Historical Archives in Philadelphia than any other single location. I thank the staff and archivists who answered my many questions, pulled dusty boxes off shelves, and copied so many pages for me. My thanks to the Chicago History Museum for offering me access to the archives of the Church Federation of Greater Chicago. Many people helped me at key points to clarify or elaborate on a number of issues in the book. They read individual chapters or the full manuscript. My apologies in advance if I have forgotten any names. The following people deserve special mention: Catherine Brekus (who read multiple iterations and drafts of different chapters), Rick Rosengarten, Margy Mitchell (who as dean fully supported an early draft of this manuscript), Paul Harvey, Tisa Wenger, Wallace Best, Judith Weisenfeld, David D. Hall, Ed Blum (who provided helpful feedback), Clark Gilpin (whose advice in the early stage of the work was invaluable), Richard Miller, Kevin Hector, Susan Schreiner, and Heather Curtis. I presented chapters from the manuscript at the American Religious History Workshop at the University of Chicago Divinity School; a University of Chicago Divinity School faculty retreat; Princeton University's American Religion workshop; Harvard Divinity School's North American Religions colloquium; as part of Harvard University's Charles Warren Center Faculty Fellows program; at gatherings of the Southern Historical Association, the American Society of Church History, and the American Academy of Religion; and in the Otts-Maloney lectureship at Davidson College (which was the first time this work took a definite form).

I still feel like I am having ongoing conversations with the late Bill Hutchison, whose seminal work on liberal Protestantism has shaped many of my earlier queries. Many thanks to friends, students, and former students whose conversations and questions helped shape this book: Erin Simmonds, Hannah Ozmun, Greg Chatterley, and Joel Brown. A special thanks, however, goes to Emily Crews, a friend and colleague, whose presence, friendship, multiple conversations, and humor have fostered the integration of my personal and intellectual life in a satisfying and meaningful way. Thanks, Emily, for reminding me, through participation in your marriage ceremony, through the birth and growth of Gus, and your return to Chicago, what true friendship means. I consider true friendships one of life's greatest pleasures and achievements.

NOTES

INTRODUCTION

1 *Obituary of Charles H. Tuttle, New York Times*, January 27, 1971.

2 Presbyterian Historical Society (hereafter PHS), RG 18 Box 56 Folder 6.

3 PHS, RG 18 Box 1 Folder 2.

4 PHS, RG 18 Box Folder 2.

5 David Hollinger claims that "ecumenical Protestantism was anything but marginal to American life during the mid-twentieth century" and that the FCC represented "the public face of Protestantism itself" up to 1950. David A. Hollinger, "After Cloven Tongues of Fire: Ecumenical Protestantism and the Modern Encounter with Diversity," *The Journal of American History* 98, no. 1 (June 2011): 23.

6 For one of the many recent studies of the Christian Right, which traces its political and social origins to the 1920s, see Daniel K. Williams, *God's Own Party: The Making of the Christian Right* (New York: Oxford University Press, 2010).

7 See Elesha J. Coffman, *The Christian Century and the Rise of the Protestant Mainline* (New York: Oxford University Press, 2013); David A. Hollinger, *After Cloven Tongues of Fire: Protestant Liberalism in Modern American History* (Princeton, NJ: Princeton University Press, 2013); and Gene Zubovich, *Before the Religious Right: Liberal Protestants, Human Rights, and the Polarization of the United States* (Philadelphia: University of Pennsylvania, 2022). Zubovich covers some of the same topics I discuss, but I provide more detail on the extended race work of the FCC over two decades, and my emphasis is on the domestic situation in the US rather than the international human rights situation that is the subject of his analysis. On the dissemination of liberal Protestant ideas in print culture in the early twentieth century, see Matthew S. Hedstrom, *The Rise of Liberal Religion: Book Culture and American Spirituality in the Twentieth Century* (New York: Oxford University Press, 2013). Following Hollinger, I prefer the term "ecumenical Christianity" or ecumenical Protestantism, because the FCC and various strands of this Protestant Christianity have emphasized ecumenism or unity in the body of Christ as central concerns of the church. The FCC, especially its Department of Race Relations, was not composed of only Protestant liberals, and the presence of African Americans and women often complicated these categories even further.

8 See William R. Hutchison, "Protestantism as Establishment," in William R. Hutchison, ed., *Between the Times: The Travail of the Protestant Establishment in America, 1900–1960* (New York: Cambridge University Press, 1989), 1–18.

9 For a further elaboration of the ecumenical vision, see Jill K. Gill, *Embattled Ecumenism: The National Council of Churches, the Vietnam War, and the Trials of the Protestant Left* (DeKalb, IL: Northern Illinois University Press, 2011), 5–6, 423–429.

10 PHS, RG 18 Box 8 Folder 21.

11 On evangelical and conservative Protestant priorities of this time, see Matthew Avery Sutton, *American Apocalypse: A History of Modern Evangelicalism* (Cambridge, MA: Belknap Press, 2014); and Frances FitzGerald, *The Evangelicals: The Struggle to Shape America* (New York: Simon & Schuster, 2017), especially chapters 4 to 6.

12 The gendered male language of brotherhood and fatherhood is recognized in this work, but I have chosen these terms because of their common usage at the time and the difficulty in finding more gender-neutral terms that would more accurately capture meanings that were historically contingent and specific. I do make reference later in this work to the heretofore neglected work of women in the Department of Race Relations. For a critical assessment of the role of women in the FCC and the Protestant establishment more generally, see Virginia Lieson Brereton, "United and Slighted: Women as Subordinated Insiders," in Hutchison, *Between the Times*, 143–167.

13 PHS, RG 18 Box 56 Folder 6.

14 Fay Botham, *Almighty God Created the Races: Christianity, Interracial Marriage, & American Law* (Chapel Hill: University of North Carolina Press, 2009), 6–8.

15 PHS, RG 18 Box 61 Folder 1.

16 On the cultural gifts movement, see Diana Selig, *Americans All: The Cultural Gifts Movement* (Cambridge, MA: Harvard University Press, 2008).

17 For more on Myrdal and these debates, see Curtis J. Evans, *The Burden of Black Religion* (New York: Oxford University Press, 2008), ch. 7; and Walter A. Jackson, *Gunnar Myrdal and America's Social Conscience: Social Engineering and Racial Liberalism, 1938–1987* (Chapel Hill: University of North Carolina Press, 1990).

18 For a fuller exploration of the ways in which liberal Protestants promoted and came to terms with religious diversity both within and beyond the Christian tradition, see David Mislin, *Saving Faith: Making Religious Pluralism an American Value at the Dawn of the Secular Age* (Ithaca, NY: Cornell University Press, 2015). Mislin also charts the early years of the FCC's work with Catholics and Jews. See also Kevin M. Schultz, *Tri-Faith America: How Catholics and Jews Held Postwar America to Its Protestant Promise* (New York: Oxford University Press, 2011), 26–35. For a slightly different and more critical approach to the tri-faith movement and how inclusive it was, see K. Healan Gaston, *Imagining Judeo-Christian*

America: Religion, Secularism, and the Redefinition of American Democracy (Chicago: University of Chicago Press, 2019).

19 Gary Gerstle, *American Crucible: Race and Nation in the Twentieth Century* (Princeton: Princeton University Press, 2001), 4–9.

20 See Edward J. Blum, *Reforging the White Republic: Race, Religion, and American Nationalism, 1865–1898* (Baton Rouge: Louisiana State University Press, 2005), 6–7. For a slightly different angle and focus on a "tri-faith" religious development that challenged "native, white Protestant supremacy" and provided an alternative, more capacious vision of the American nation, see Kevin M. Schultz, *Tri-Faith America*, especially chapter 1, for the origins of this vision.

21 Thomas J. Sugrue, *Sweet Land of Liberty: The Forgotten Struggle for Civil Rights in the North* (New York: Random House, 2008), xix–xx.

22 Ibid., 7–8. More specifically, I build and elaborate on David Mislin's conclusion that, by the 1920s, liberal Protestants' "enthusiasm for pluralism expanded beyond religious diversity and into the realm of racial and ethnic differences." See Mislin, *Saving Faith*, 159.

23 David W. Wills, "An Enduring Distance: Black Americans and the Establishment," in Hutchinson, *Between the Times*, 172.

24 James F. Findlay, *Church People in the Struggle: The National Council of Churches and the Black Freedom Movement, 1950–1970* (New York: Oxford University Press, 1993), 18–19.

25 David L. Chappell, *A Stone of Hope: Prophetic Religion and the Death of Jim Crow* (Chapel Hill: University of North Carolina Press, 2004), 179.

26 Chappell does note that recent scholarship indicates that Niebuhr was criticizing liberalism, especially liberal theology, from within. But even with this concession, the thrust of his discussion of Niebuhr, particularly Niebuhr's rejection of utopianism and his emphasis on coercion as central to achieving a measure of justice, is that Niebuhr rightly chided and parted company with naïve and optimistic liberals. In general, Chappell's depiction is a caricature of the strand of liberal ecumenical theology espoused by the FCC, where the concern with race in particular stripped away any illusions about easy or inevitable change. In accord with Chappell, however, I try to show that like his liberals, FCC leaders learned from their experiences and became more chastened and determined to produce social change after years of setbacks and hardships.

27 See Dennis Dickerson, "African American Religious Intellectuals and the Theological Foundations for the Civil Rights Movement," *Church History* 74, no. 2 (June 2005). Haynes is not among those covered in Dickerson's essay, though I think his social thought and reformist projects were expressions of Social Gospel activism. For another perspective on Social Gospel thought among black religious leaders from the 1930s to the 1950s, see Gary Dorrien, *Breaking White Supremacy: Martin Luther King, Jr. and the Black Social Gospel* (New Haven, CT: Yale University Press, 2018), especially chapters 1 and 2.

28 Benjamin E. Mays, "The Church Amidst Ethnic and Racial Tensions," in Davis W. Houck and David E. Dixon, eds., *Rhetoric, Religion, and the Civil Rights Movement* (Waco, TX: Baylor University Press, 2006), 55–64.

29 Mays, Haynes, Channing H. Tobias, and other black leaders worked within predominantly white religious organizations like the YMCA, which often served as a stepping-stone to a more prestigious career. For more on Tobias in particular, see Nina Mjagkij, *Light in the Darkness: African Americans and the YMCA, 1852–1946* (Lexington: The University Press of Kentucky, 1994).

30 For more on Mays, see Barbara Dianne Savage, *Your Spirits Walk Beside Us: The Politics of Black Religion* (Cambridge, MA: Harvard University Press, 2008), ch. 5; and Randal Maurice Jelks, *Benjamin Elijah Mays, Schoolmaster of the Movement: A Biography* (Chapel Hill: University of North Carolina Press, 2012).

31 Sugrue, *Sweet Land of Liberty*, xxii–xxiv.

32 On this point more generally, see Christopher H. Evans, *The Social Gospel in American Religion: A History* (New York: New York University Press, 2017), ch. 5, "Since Rauschenbusch What? The Social Gospel Between the World Wars."

33 I have taken the expression "faith in the possibility of a new social order" from Walter Rauschenbusch, *Christianity and the Social Crisis* (Louisville, KY: Westminster/John Knox Press, 1991 [1907]), 349.

CHAPTER 1. A PROTESTANT THEOLOGY OF BROTHERHOOD

1 PHS, RG 18 Box 57 Folder 3.

2 Robert T. Handy, *A Christian America: Protestant Hopes and Historical Realities* (New York: Oxford University Press, 1971), 131. For Speer's role in the theological divisions of his time and his more inclusive views of race compared to some of his Presbyterian contemporaries, see Bradley J. Longfield, *The Presbyterian Controversy: Fundamentalists, Modernists, and Moderates* (New York: Oxford University Press, 1991), ch. 8.

3 Handy, *A Christian America*, 129–132; and William R. Hutchison, *Errand to the World: American Protestant Thought and Foreign Missions* (Chicago: University of Chicago Press, 1987), 121–123, 147.

4 PHS, RG 18 Box 57 Folder 3.

5 As Robert Schneider also notes, one of the original functions of the FCC was to "demonstrate the actual unity, despite obvious diversity, of American Protestant Christianity." See Schneider's "Voices of Many Waters: Church Federation in the Twentieth Century," in Hutchison, *Between the Times*, 105. This ecumenical impulse for unity was a factor in the later (in the 1920s) turn to race and the treatment of African Americans, issues that were an obvious source of division in the churches.

6 On this point about the transformation of Christianity, see Markku Ruotsila, *The Origins of Christian Anti-Internationalism: Conservative Evangelicals and the League of Nations* (Washington, DC: Georgetown University Press, 2008), 12–13.

7 See Brook Thomas, ed., *Plessy v. Ferguson: A Brief History with Documents* (Boston: Bedford/St. Martin's, 1997), 51.

8 See George Fredrickson, *The Black Image in the White Mind: The Debate on Afro-American Character and Destiny, 1817–1914* (Middletown, CT: Wesleyan University Press, 1987 [1971]), 320–321. See also Charles A. Lofgren, *The Plessy Case: A Legal-Historical Interpretation* (New York: Oxford University Press, 1987), ch. 5. Although a plethora of more recent scholarship exists on race relations in this period, some of which I cite in footnotes below, I still find these two older works useful as summaries of the points that I make in this paragraph.

9 George Frederickson, *Racism: A Short History* (Princeton: Princeton University Press, 2002), 1–13.

10 Ibid.

11 Blum, *Reforging the White Republic.*

12 Ralph Luker, *The Social Gospel in Black and White: American Racial Reform, 1885–1912* (Chapel Hill and London: University of North Carolina Press, 1991), ch. 10.

13 *Ibid.*, 268, 301–310. See also James M. McPherson, *The Abolitionist Legacy: From Reconstruction to the NAACP* (Princeton, NJ: Princeton University Press, 1995 [1975]), 345–353.

14 See Fay Botham, *"Almighty God Created the Races": Christianity, Interracial Marriage, & American Law* (Chapel Hill: University of North Carolina Press, 2009); and Jane Dailey, ed., *The Age of Jim Crow: A Norton Casebook in History* (New York: W. W. Norton & Company, Inc., 2009), xxvi–xxxv.

15 F. Ernest Johnson and Arthur Holt, *Christian Ideals in Industry* (New York: The Methodist Book Concern, 1924), 71.

16 On Holt, see Jacob Dorn, "The Rural Ideal and Agrarian Realities: Arthur E. Holt and the Vision of a Decentralized America in the Interwar Years," *Church History* 52, no. 1 (March 1983), 50–65.

17 C. Howard Hopkins, *The Rise of the Social Gospel in American Protestantism, 1865–1915* (New Haven, CT: Yale University Press, 1967 [1940]), 126.

18 Washington Gladden, *Ruling Ideas of the Present Age* (Boston and New York: Houghton, Mifflin and Company, 1895), 33.

19 Ibid., 34–35.

20 Gladden, *Applied Christianity: Moral Aspects of Social Questions* 8th ed. (Boston and New York: Houghton, Mifflin and Company, 1894), 148.

21 Ibid., 170–171.

22 For more on Gladden's influence, see William R. Hutchison, *The Modernist Impulse in American Protestantism* (New York: Oxford University Press, 1976), 76–78, 116; and Christopher Evans, *The Social Gospel*, 32–35. See also Gary Dorrien, *The Making of American Liberal Theology: Imagining Progress Religion, 1805–1900* (Louisville, KY: Westminster John Knox Press, 2001), 304–314, 324–334. Dorrien provides a helpful summary of Gladden's views and actions on race. My discussion

of Gladden's theological writings on brotherhood necessarily suggests a more positive understanding of his view of African Americans and race relations because it deals with his ideals, but my analysis is not meant to downplay his complicated actions and social engagement on race. The point I hope to convey is that this theological contribution of brotherhood was a challenge to dominant theories of race such as the theology of racial segregation in the South and the ascendant scientific racism in much of the North and in university contexts.

23 On Gladden's presence at the planning conference for the FCC, see David Mislin, *Washington Gladden's Church: The Minister Who Made Modern American Protestantism* (Lanham, MD: Rowman & Littlefield, 2019), 136.

24 Reverdy C. Ransom, "The Race Problem in a Christian State, 1906," in Milton C. Sernett, ed., *African American Religious History: A Documentary Witness*, 2nd ed. (Durham, NC: Duke University Press, 1999), 338. See also Robert Gregg, *Sparks from the Anvil of Oppression: Philadelphia's African Methodists and Southern Migrants, 1890–1940* (Philadelphia: Temple University Press, 1993), 95–98, 242. For diametrically opposite white segregationist readings of the second half of Acts 17:26 ("and [God] hath determined the times before appointed, and the boundaries of their habitation"), see Jane Dailey, "Sex, Segregation, and the Sacred after *Brown*," *Journal of American History* 91, no. 1 (June 2004), 122–125. More generally, see Paul Harvey, *Bounds of their Habitation: Race and Religion in American History* (Lanham, MD: Rowman & Littlefield, 2017).

25 Ransom, "The Race Problem," 338. The reference to the wall of partition was a quotation from Ephesians 2:14–16, the part of which cited by Ransom was: "that He might reconcile both unto God in one body by the cross, having slain the enmity thereby, so making peace."

26 Ibid., 342?

27 Ibid.

28 Ibid.

29 For more on Grimké, see Mark Perry, *Lift Up Thy Voice: The Grimké Family's Journey from Slaveholders to Civil Rights Leaders* (New York: Penguin Group, 2001); Louis B. Weeks, III, "Racism, World War I, and the Christian Life: Francis J. Grimké in the Nation's Capital," *Journal of Presbyterian History* 51, no. 4 (Winter 1973), 471–488; Dickson D. Bruce, Jr., *Archibald* Grimké*: Portrait of a Black Independent* (Baton Rouge: Louisiana State University Press, 1993), 9–28; and Henry Justin Ferris, "Francis James Grimké: Portrait of a Black Puritan," (dissertation, Yale University, 1970).

30 Carter G. Woodson, ed., *The Works of Francis J.* Grimké, vol. 1 (Washington, DC: Associated Publishers, Inc, 1942), 447–448.

31 Edward J. Blum, "'O God of a Godless Land': Northern African American Challenges to White Christian Nationhood, 1865–1906," in Edward J. Blum and W. Scott Poole, eds., *Vale of Tears: New Essays on Religion and Reconstruction* (Macon, GA: Mercer University Press, 2005), 93–111. See also Blum, *Reforging the*

White Republic, 244–249. On black leaders and arguments for a distinctive black social gospel, see Gary Dorrien, *The New Abolition: W. E. B. Du Bois and the Black Social Gospel* (New Haven, CT: Yale University Press, 2015).

32 See Edward J. Blum, *W. E. B. Du Bois: American Prophet* (Philadelphia: University of Pennsylvania Press, 2007), especially ch. 4.

33 Kelly Miller, "Religion as the Solvent of the Race Problem" (1908; reprint, *Race Adjustment/The Everlasting Stain* [New York: Arno Press, 1968]), 133–134.

34 Willard B. Gatewood, *Aristocrats of Color: The Black Elite, 1880–1920* (Fayetteville: University of Arkansas Press, 2000 [1990]), 296–297.

35 David W. Wills, gen. ed., African American Religion: A Documentary History Project, Part 3, Roster 10, aardoc.sites.amherst.edu.

36 See Michael Kazin, *A Godly Hero: A Life of William Jennings Bryan* (New York: Alfred A. Knopf, 2006), 93–94, 227–228.

37 *New York Age* 39, no. 14 (December 19, 1925).

38 On how socially conservative African American and white fundamentalist communities wrestled with the challenges of modernity and racial issues in the interwar years, see Mary Beth Swetnam Matthews, *Doctrine and Race: African American Evangelicals and Fundamentalism Between the Wars* (Tuscaloosa: The University of Alabama Press, 2017); and Daniel R. Bare, *Black Fundamentalism: Conservative Christianity and Racial Identity in the Segregation Era* (New York: New York University Press, 2021).

39 Ronald C. White, Jr., *Liberty and Justice for All: Racial Reform and the Social Gospel* (New York: Harper & Row, 1991), 247–249.

40 For more on the Great Migration and racial violence in particular in the postwar period, see Eric Arnesen, *Black Protest and the Great Migration: A Brief History with Documents* (Boston: Bedford/St. Martin's, 2003), 29–35.

41 See Alfred L. Brophy, *Reconstructing the Dreamland: The Tulsa Riot of 1921: Race, Reparations, and Reconciliation* (New York: Oxford University Press, 2002).

42 PHS, RG 18 Box 57 Folder 3.

43 For a classic statement of the central themes of social Christianity, see Hopkins, *The Rise of the Social Gospel in American Protestantism, 1865–1915*, 105–117. For a positive assessment of Social Gospel leaders' take on race and their appreciation of ethnic diversity, see William R. Hutchison, *Religious Pluralism in America: The Contentious History of a Founding Ideal* (New Haven, CT: Yale University Press, 2008), 85. See also Christopher Evans, *The Social Gospel*.

44 PHS, RG 18 Box 57 Folder 3.

45 Ibid.

46 Ibid.

47 Ibid.

48 Ibid.

49 For helpful analyses, see Lynn Dumenil, *The Modern Temper: American Culture and Society in the 1920s* (New York: Hill and Wang, 1995), 3–13; and Erica J. Ryan,

When the World Broke in Two: The Roaring Twenties and the Dawn of America's Culture Wars (Denver, CO: Praeger, 2018).

50 Stanley Corben, "The Assault on Victorianism in the Twentieth Century," in *Victorian America*, ed. Daniel Walker Howe (Philadelphia: University of Pennsylvania Press, 1984), 169.

51 See also Carl Degler, *In Search of Human Nature: The Decline and Revival of Darwinism in American Social Thought* (New York: Oxford University Press, 1991), especially section 2, "The Sovereignty of Culture."

52 For a helpful analysis, see Dumenil, *Modern Temper*.

53 On the theme of church federation and changing the nation, see Robert A. Schneider, "Voice of Many Waters: Church Federation in the Twentieth Century," in Hutchison, *Between the Times*, 95–121.

54 Kelly J. Baker, *Gospel According to the Klan: The KKK's Appeal to Protestant America, 1915–1930* (Lawrence: University Press of Kansas, 2011), 11. For a critical analysis of recent scholarship on the Klan and an overview of its influence in the 1920s, see Thomas P. Pegram, *One Hundred Percent American: The Rebirth and Decline of the Ku Klux Klan in the 1920s* (Chicago: Ivan R. Dee, 2011). Two older works I have also found useful: John Higham, *Strangers in the Land: Patterns of Nativism, 1860–1925* (New Brunswick, NJ: Rutgers University Press, 2004 [1955]), ch. 10; and Kenneth T. Jackson, *The Ku Klux Klan in the City, 1915–1930* (New York: Oxford University Press, 1967).

55 For more on this ideal of America as a unified white Protestant nation, see Allan J. Lichtman, *White Protestant Nation: The Rise of the American Conservative Movement* (New York: Atlantic Monthly Press, 2008), 1–4.

56 Baker, *Gospel According to the Klan*, 8–9.

57 Diana Selig, *Americans All: The Cultural Gifts Movement* (Cambridge, MA: Harvard University Press, 2008). Rachel Davis DuBois, a Quaker, described by Selig as one of the most prominent champions of anti-prejudice efforts in the schools during the 1920s and 1930s, was one example of the connection between cultural gifts proponents and the FCC. For a time, DuBois edited the *Interracial Newsletter*, the main publication of the FCC's Department of Race Relations, though not all of its collections represented the formal position of the FCC. She gave reports about her work in schools before the Church Women's Committee in 1934 and became an official member of this Committee in 1938. See PHS, RG 18 Box 56 Folders 4 and 12. For more on DuBois, see Selig, *Americans All*, ch. 3; and Allan W. Austin, *Quaker Brotherhood: Interracial Activism and the American Friends Service Committee, 1917–1950* (Urbana: University of Illinois Press, 2012), 26–27, 32–33.

58 For more on the ways in which conservative and fundamentalist Protestants rejected the ecumenical vision of the FCC, especially the FCC's attempt to work with those outside the Christian faith in forming the United Nations and developing human rights, see Markku Ruotsila, *The Origins of Christian*

Anti-Internationalism: Conservative Evangelicals and the League of Nations (Washington, DC: Georgetown University Press, 2008), 171–180. See also William Inboden, *Religion and American Foreign Policy, 1945–1960: The Soul of Containment* (New York: Cambridge University Press, 2008), 30–38, 81–87; and Gene Zubovich, *Before the Religious Right: Liberal Protestants, Human Rights, and the Polarization of the United States* (Philadelphia: University of Pennsylvania Press, 2022), ch. 5.

59 On the nature of these debates in the context of the 1920s, see George M. Marsden, *Fundamentalism and American Culture: The Shaping of Twentieth-Century Evangelicalism, 1870–1925* (New York: Oxford University Press, 1980), 164–184.

60 PHS, RG 18 Box 59 Folder 22.

61 Ibid.

CHAPTER 2. "A STAIN UPON OUR NATIONAL HONOR"

1 PHS, RG 18 Box 57 Folder 3.

2 On the NAACP's realization that an attack on lynching would in part be a "contest of language," see Philip Dray, *At the Hands of Persons Unknown: The Lynching of Black America* (New York: Random House, 2002), 177. For a comparative treatment of lynching in two states, see W. Fitzhugh Brundage, *Lynching in the New South: Georgia and Virginia, 1880–1930* (Urbana: University of Illinois Press, 1993).

3 PHS, RG 18 Box 8 Folder 22. On Roosevelt's tepid support for anti-lynching bills and the power of white southern senators and representatives in Congress fiercely opposed to any challenge to Jim Crow laws, see Dray, *At the Hands of Person Unknown*, 356–362; and Ira Katznelson, *Fear Itself: The New Deal and the Origins of Our Time* (New York: Liveright, 2013), 161–182.

4 On Truman and his policies against lynching, see Dray, *At the Hands of Persons Unknown*, 383–387.

5 PHS, RG 18 Box 59 Folder 22.

6 Hollinger, *After Cloven Tongues of Fire: Protestant Liberalism in Modern American History*, 22–23.

7 On the significance of the Second World War (and the ensuing Cold War) as a "transition point" and a catalyst for international attention to American racism, see Mary L. Dudziak, *Cold War and Civil Rights: Race and the Image of American Democracy* (Princeton, NJ: Princeton University Press, 2000), 7.

8 On church-state concerns, see John A. Hutchison, "We Are Not Divided: A Critical and Historical Study of the Federal Council of the Churches of Christ in America," (PhD diss., Columbia University, 1941), 90–98; and William M. King, "The Reform Establishment and the Ambiguities of Influence," in Hutchison, *Between the Times*,132–134.

9 On the fate of the Dyer bill, see Robert Zangrando, *The NAACP Crusade Against Lynching, 1909–1950* (Philadelphia: Temple University Press, 1980), ch. 3. I have

been unable to find discussions of the Dyer bill in FCC archives. Given the FCC's origin in 1908, the infrastructure was certainly in place to debate the merits of the bill. It seems reasonable to assume that the FCC was goaded to address racial issues in its early years by black churches, southern representatives, and external events such as the dislocations of the Great War and the migration of blacks from the South.

10 For more on attempts by southern moderates and liberals (most of whom rejected federal legislation and many of whom were church members) to end lynching, see Morton Sosna, *In Search of the Silent South: Southern Liberals and the Race Issue* (New York: Columbia University Press, 1977), 30–41. For a negative assessment of southern liberals, and a judgment about the Commission on Interracial Cooperation as a moderate force, see John Egerton, *Speak Now Against the Day: The Generation Before the Civil Rights Movement in the South* (New York: Alfred A. Knopf, 1994), especially 42–50, 301–307; and David L. Chappell, *Inside Agitators: White Southerners in the Civil Rights Movement* (Baltimore: John Hopkins University Press, 1996), pt. 1. For a slightly more favorable view of the CIC, see Diane Selig, *Americans All*, ch. 5, "A New Generation in the South."

11 PHS, RG 18 Box 59 Folder 20. The FCC relied mostly on the *Negro Year Book* for these figures, which was edited by Monroe Work, Director of Records and Statistics at Tuskegee Institute. Tuskegee was the principal source of reliable lynching statistics. The FCC also cited the NAACP's *Thirty Years of Lynching in the United States, 1889–1918* as a source. For recent attempts to get accurate numbers of the lynchings that occurred in the South and in the entire nation, see Stewart E. Tolnay and E. M. Beck, *A Festival of Violence: An Analysis of Southern Lynchings, 1882–1930* (Urbana: University of Illinois Press, 1995); and Dray, *At the Hands of Persons Unknown*, vii–ix. For debates over the very definition of lynching, see Christopher Waldrep, *The Many Faces of Judge Lynch: Extralegal Violence and Punishment in America* (New York: Palgrave MacMillan, 2002), 1–12, and especially ch. 7.

12 PHS, RG 18 Box 59 Folder 20.

13 On the ritualized nature of spectacle lynchings, see Amy Louise Wood, *Lynching and Spectacle: Witnessing Racial Violence in America, 1890–1940* (Chapel Hill: University of North Carolina Press, 2009).

14 PHS, RG 18 Box 59 Folder 20.

15 Ibid. This comment was actually made during a personal visit that Samuel McCrea Cavert, general secretary of the FCC, had made to India in 1917. Cavert related in an article, "Will the Christian Conscience End the Lynching Evil?" (*Federal Council Bulletin*, August-September, 1919) that, upon visiting Tagore at his home in Bolpur, "To my question as to his attitude toward the work of Christian missionaries in India, the poet replied: 'I received yesterday from America a newspaper which described the burning of two black men by a mob. Don't you think it would be well to practice brotherhood at home, at least in such

elemental matters as protecting human life, before you presume to teach brotherhood in Asia?'" About which Cavert wrote, "What would one answer to such a question as that?" See PHS, RG 18 Box 80 Folder 16. Mark Twain wrote a moving piece two decades earlier, urging American missionaries in China to come back to the United States "into the lynching field" to Christianize white Americans. It was his satiric take on exporting Christianity to other nations when Americans had so many problems at home. See Mark Twain, "The United States of Lyncherdom," 1901, in Mark Twain, *Mark Twain: Collected Tales, Sketches, Speeches, & Essays, 1891–1910* (New York: Literary Classics of the United States, 1992), 479–486. For a helpful essay on Tagore's popularity among American and English suffragists, see Kathi Kern, "Spiritual Border-Crossings in the U.S. Women's Rights Movement," in Leigh E. Schmidt and Sally M. Promey, eds., *American Religious Liberalism* (Bloomington: Indiana University Press, 2012), 162–181.

16 For a helpful introduction to and compilation of Wells's anti-lynching works, see Jacqueline Jones Royster, ed., *Southern Horrors and Other Writings: The Anti-Lynching Campaign of Ida B. Wells, 1892–1900* (Boston: Bedford Books, 1997).

17 PHS, RG 18 Box 59 Folder 20. It is estimated that at least one hundred fifty women were lynched, and thousands more assaulted by white mobs, in the South between 1880 and 1965, the majority occurring before 1930. About one hundred thirty of these women were African Americans. See Crystal N. Feimster, *Southern Horrors: Women and the Politics of Rape and Lynching* (Cambridge, MA: Harvard University Press, 2009), ch. 6.

18 PHS, RG 18 Box 59 Folder 20. On the role of newspaper editors in inciting white lynch mobs, see Waldrep, *The Many Faces of Judge Lynch*, 128–131.

19 PHS, RG 18 Box 59 Folder 20.

20 For one example among many, see "Honor Roll of States Free of Lynching in 1931," PHS, RG 18 Box 60 Folder 1.

21 PHS, RG 18 Box 60 Folder 11. Sixteen lynchings had occurred in 1927. Perhaps because Haynes was writing at the very beginning of 1928, the most recent statistics had not come out on the previous year.

22 PHS, RG 18 Box 60 Folder 11.

23 Ibid.

24 Ibid.

25 Dray, *At the Hands of Persons Unknown*, 303–362. On the formation of the ASWPL, see Jacqueline Dowd Hall, *Revolt Against Chivalry: Jessie Daniel Ames and the Women's Campaign Against Lynching* (New York: Columbia University Press, 1979), ch. 6. On the origins of the IDL and the work of Communist groups in the South, see Glenda Gilmore, *Defying Dixie: The Radical Roots of Civil Rights, 1919–1950* (New York: W. W. Norton & Co., 2008), ch. 2.

26 Brundage, *Lynching in the New South*, 245–251; and Dray, *At the Hands of Persons Unknown*, 303–304.

27 See Wood, *Lynching and Spectacle*, 262.

28 Though some of its investigators pointed to social and economic issues as the cause of lynchings, the FCC officially represented racial violence against blacks as a moral problem—as a stain upon the nation's moral character.

29 PHS, RG 18 Box 59 Folder 20.

30 Ibid.

31 Ibid.

32 A long tradition of vigilantism and even violent popular sovereignty has been noted by scholars as powerful forces in local communities in the United States, and partly explains the justifications for lynchings. The demand for public executions persisted in the South into the twentieth century. See Wood, *Lynching and Spectacle*, 23–33; Michael J. Pfeifer, *Rough Justice: Lynching and American Society, 1874–1947* (Urbana: University of Illinois Press, 2004), ch. 4; and Margaret Vandiver, *Lethal Punishment: Lynchings and Legal Executions in the South* (New Brunswick, NJ: Rutgers University Press, 2006), ch. 6.

33 PHS, RG 18 Box 59 Folder 20.

34 Ibid.

35 Ibid.

36 Ibid.

37 Ibid.

38 Mitchell would run on a Socialist ticket for governor of Maryland in 1934. He lost that race, garnering a tiny minority of votes.

39 Ibid.

40 Mitchell noted later in his life that local people carped that a "heathen had come among them and scolded them." See Broadus Mitchell, August 14 and 15, 1977, Interview B-0024, Southern Oral History Program Collection, #4007, Chapel Hill. On the linkage between race, radicalism, and Communism by white southerners, see Jeff Woods, *Black Struggle, Red Scare: Segregation and Anti-Communism in the South, 1948–1968* (Baton Rouge: Louisiana State University Press, 2004).

41 *Congressional Record*, 73rd Congress, 2nd Session, (February 20–21, 1934), 171.

42 *Cong. Rec.*, 73rd Cong., 2nd sess., (February 20–21, 1934), 171-73.

43 The lynching of Claude Neal is regarded as the end of spectacle lynching, even though the gruesome deaths of Roosevelt Townes and Robert Mc Daniels, who were whipped with a chain and tortured with the flames from gasoline blow-torches before being burned alive and shot, respectively, took place in Duck Hill, Mississippi in 1937, at the hands of a crowd of three to four hundred. Neal was tortured in the backwoods over a period of ten hours by a mob of one hundred white men, who cut off his genitals and forced him to eat them. After he was killed by a blast from a shotgun, his body was paraded before a much larger crowd who dragged, mutilated, and urinated on his lifeless body before it was hung on a tree. The kidnapping charge came about because he was taken across

state lines from local authorities and transported from Alabama to Florida, where he was murdered. See Grace Elizabeth Hale, *Making Whiteness: The Culture of Segregation in the South, 1890–1940* (New York: Vintage Books, 1998), 222–227; and Dray, *The Lynching of Black America*, 344–354, 359–361.

44 PHS, RG 18 Box 59 Folder 22.

45 PHS, RG 18 Box 59 Folder 23. By relying on already established networks to communicate information quickly, the FCC engaged in tactics similar to the women of the ASWPL. See Dowd, *Revolt Against Chivalry*, 239–240.

46 PHS, RG 18 Box 59 Folder 23.

47 Ibid.

48 For a look at the male "decision makers," which neglects the activity of women, especially in race work, see Robert A. Schneider, "Voice of Many Waters: Church Federation in the Twentieth Century," in Hutchison, *Between the Times*, 104.

49 PHS, RG 18 Box 55 Folder 1. The resolution on restrictive covenants read: "The Federal Council of the Churches of Christ in America deplores the use of restrictive covenants based on race, which is so widespread in our country, because it is a violation of the Gospel of love and human brotherhood destroying the dignity of human personality and Christian Justice." On the legal struggle against restrictive covenants as "the beginning, not the end, of the battle against housing segregation," and responses to the Supreme Court decision *Shelley v. Kraemer* (1948), which made restrictive covenants legally unenforceable, see Thomas J. Sugrue, *Sweet Land of Liberty: The Forgotten Struggle for Civil Rights in the North* (New York: Random House, 2008), 207–220.

50 PHS, RG 18 Box 56 Folder 1.

51 See Steven F. Lawson, ed., *To Secure These Rights: The Report of President Harry S Truman's Committee on Civil Rights* (Boston: Bedford/St. Martin's, 2004), 52.

52 Lawson, *To Secure These Rights*, 61.

53 Ibid., 129–130.

54 Ibid., 127.

55 For more on how the "treatment of African Americans became a matter fraught with international implications" in the Cold War years, see Lawson, *To Secure These Rights*, 9.

CHAPTER 3. RACE RELATIONS SUNDAYS

1 PHS, RG 18 Box 58 Folder 6.

2 Ibid.

3 Ibid.

4 On the ordering of time and the Christian calendar, I have found the following essay on a different historical context helpful: Leigh E. Schmidt, "Time, Celebration, and the Christian Year in Eighteenth-Century Evangelicalism," in Mark Noll, David W. Bebbington, and George A. Rawlyk, eds., *Evangelicalism: Comparative Studies of Popular Protestantism in North America, the British Isles,*

and Beyond, 1700–1900 (New York: Oxford University Press, 1994), 90–109. Especially relevant to my analysis of the FCC's Christian calendar are the questions of how sacred times/holidays are named and distinguished from mundane occasions, and how religious and moral identities are forged and maintained through distinctive calendrical observances.

5 PHS, RG 18 Box 57 Folder 3.

6 PHS, RG 18 Box 58 Folder 6.

7 David W. Wills, "An Enduring Distance: Black Americans and the Establishment," in William R. Hutchison, ed. *Between the Times: The Travail of the Protestant Establishment in America, 1900–1960* (Cambridge, England: Cambridge University Press, 1989), 172.

8 Regarding matters of race and racism, I have not settled on any singular term, but I have tried to capture the terms or meaning of race as it was understood in the early twentieth century. Hence my use of various terms, including "racial division," "racial oppression," and "race relations," among others.

9 Ibid., 173–175. For more details on Haynes's life, see Daniel Perlman, "Stirring the White Conscience: The Life of George Edmund Haynes," PhD diss., New York University, 1972; and Samuel Kelton Roberts, "Crucible for a Vision: The Work of George Edmund Haynes and the Commission on Race Relations, 1922–1947," PhD diss., Columbia University, 1974. For an interesting mix of personal and academic perspectives on Haynes's life, see Bruce D. Haynes and Syma Solovitch, *Down the Up Staircase: Three Generations of a Harlem Family* (New York: Columbia University Press, 2017), 26–64. Bruce D. Haynes, a sociologist at the University of California, Davis, is the grandson of George Edmund Haynes. I initiated email contact with Bruce on January 24, 2019, and we then spoke on the phone about his memories of his grandfather and to get his professional view of his grandfather's contributions to social science.

10 George Edmund Haynes, *The Trend of the Races* (New York: Council of Women for Home Missions and Missionary Education Movement of the United States and Canada, 1922), 19.

11 Haynes, *Trend of the Races*, 21.

12 Ibid., 142–143.

13 Ibid., 141.

14 Ibid., 21.

15 Ibid., 90.

16 Ibid., 166–167. Though he did not cite it directly, it seems that Haynes was alluding to Peter Kropotkin's *Mutual Aid: A Factor in Evolution*. The work, though originally published in 1902, had gone through a second edition by 1914. Kropotkin rejected what he regarded as an article of faith among Darwinists that competition and a bitter struggle for existence within species were the primary means of existence and survival for humans and animals. He based his conclusions on his own travels through eastern Siberia and Northern Manchuria.

Kropotkin had read widely in major books and articles on Darwinism. He was a leading critic of Social Darwinism. Kropotkin proposed mutual aid as a chief factor in evolution, which he argued had been overlooked or trivialized by most Darwinists. However, this Russian anarchist's political views were much more radical than Haynes and other social moderates were willing to entertain. See Peter Kropotkin, *Mutual Aid: A Factor of Evolution* (London: Penguin Books, 1972 [1917 edition]), 17–18, 23–24, and the introduction to this edition for background on Kropotkin's work. On sociability, cooperation, and altruism as biological and social imperatives from the perspective of evolutionary theorists who were critics of Social Darwinism, see Richard Hofstadter, *Social Darwinism in American Thought* Revised Edition (Boston: Beacon Press, 1955), 90–98.

17 *Trend of the Races*, 169, 170–179.

18 Ibid., 183. This statement of black insight into the lives of whites is reminiscent of W. E. B. Du Bois's claim about blacks seeing "in and through" white Americans. See Du Bois, "The Souls of White Folks" (1910), in *W. E. B. Du Bois: Writings* (New York: Library of America, 1987), 923. For a strong case for the influence of Du Bois on Haynes, see Haynes and Solovitch, *Down the Up Staircase*, 26.

19 *Trend of the Races*, 183.

20 William Graham Sumner, *Folkways: A Study of the Sociological Importance of Usages, Manners, Customs, Mores, and Morals* (New York: Dover Publications, Inc., 1959 [1906]), 3.

21 Ibid., 2–3.

22 Sumner, *Folkways*, 3–26. See also Daniel Perlman, "Stirring the White Conscience: The Life of George Edmund Haynes," PhD diss., Columbia University, 1972, 24–30. Perlman writes, "These ideas in Sumner's lectures impressed Haynes, and he incorporated the terms 'folkways' and 'mores' into his own vocabulary. Years later, in explaining the persistence of segregation and discrimination, Haynes, in phrases reminiscent of Sumner, talked of the 'persistence of folkways long after the conditions out of which they were produced have changed'" (28).

23 Ronald White, *Liberty and Justice*, 251.

24 George Edmund Haynes, "Changing Racial Attitudes and Customs," *Phylon* 2, no. 1 (1st Quarter 1941), 28. See also *Trend of the Races*, 19–20. This emphasis on pleasurable experiences and friendly contact was an anticipation of "contact theory," which became prominent among social psychologists in the 1950s and thereafter. For a helpful discussion and a positive appraisal of contact theory in the historical context of black/white interactions during the Reconstruction period, see Blum, *Reforging the White Republic*, 60–76. For a less sanguine interpretation of interracial contacts during the period Blum examines, see Evans, *Burden of Black Religion*, 63–79.

25 PHS, RG 18 Box 58 Folder 6.

26 David M. Reimers, *White Protestantism and the Negro* (New York: Oxford University Press, 1965), 112–113.

27 On these discussions, see Carol Anderson, *Eyes Off the Prize: The United Nations and the African American Struggle for Human Rights, 1944–1955* (Cambridge, England: Cambridge University Press, 2003), 18–21.

28 Haynes, *Trend of the Races*, 168.

29 For a general overview of social scientific conceptions of race in the early twentieth century, see Carl N. Degler, *In Search of Human Nature: The Decline and Revival of Darwinism in American Social Thought* (New York: Oxford University Press, 1991), 14–25.

30 Vernon J. Williams, Jr., *From Caste to a Minority: Changing Attitudes of American Sociologists Toward Afro-Americans, 1896–1945* (Westport, CT: Greenwood Press, 1989), 143–145. See also Fred H. Matthews, *Quest for an American Sociology: Robert E. Park and the Chicago School* (Montreal: McGill-Queen's University Press, 1977), 76–82, and ch. 6. Interestingly, Williams quotes E. Franklin Frazier, who studied with Park, as saying that Park's theory of race relations "contained a fatalism inherent in Sumner's concept of mores" (144). My reading of Sumner's *Folkways* and Haynes's appropriation of Sumner's work indicates that there was no fatalism "inherent" in his notion of mores and folkways. For a brief discussion on this point about fatalism in Sumner's work, from an older but still significant book, see Richard Hofstadter, *Social Darwinism in American Thought*, 64–65.

31 *Trend of the Races*, 20.

32 PHS, RG 18 Box 61 Folder 14.

33 Ibid.

34 Ibid.

35 PHS, RG 18 Box 61 Folder 14.

36 Ibid. I have tried to locate this program to no effect. The records of First Methodist and some of the papers of William Seamon are located at DePauw University. I was deeply disappointed that the records contained only a passing reference to the observance of Race Relations Sunday in 1926. Despite my asking the archivists to help with the search, I was unable to find any more information on this observance. Seamon was actively promoting a Social Gospel form of Christian practice at his "institutional church," and had a vibrant downtown ministry. He was also noted for his work among the black population in the city. See MC 116 (City Methodist Church, Gary Indiana), DePauw University, Greencastle, Indiana.

37 PHS, RG 18 Box 61 Folder 14. The "recent report" was a reference to the Meriam Report on "The Conditions Among the Indians." It chronicled poverty and ill-health among Native Americans, underscoring the failure of the Bureau of Indian Affairs' programs. For one angle on this period, see Frederick E. Hoxie, ed., *Talking Back to Civilization: Indian Voices from the Progressive Era* (Boston: Bedford/St. Martin's, 2001).

38 PHS, RG 18 Box 61 Folder 1.

39 This was certainly hopeful thinking given that many conservative Protestants and confessional denominations maintained a skepticism of the FCC from its inception. Missouri Synod Lutherans and Southern Baptists kept their distance, and a newly emerging evangelical coalition was hostile to the FCC's social and racial projects.

40 Ibid.

41 Ibid. The Chicago Church Federation listed twenty-five religious leaders at this conference, including Haynes and Shailer Mathews, former dean of the University of Chicago Divinity School. See Church Federation of Greater Chicago (CFGC), Box 65, Folder, Federal Council of Churches, at the Chicago History Museum, Chicago, IL.

42 See also, *Federal Council Bulletin*, April 1940, in PHS, RG 18 Box 61 Folder 1.

43 PHS, RG 18 Box 61 Folder 1.

44 Ibid..

45 For more on brotherhood week, the good will movement, and the NCCJ, see Benny Kraut, "A Wary Collaboration: Jews, Catholics, and the Goodwill Movement," in Hutchison, *Between the Times*, 193–230; Wendy L. Wall, *Inventing the "American Way": The Politics of Consensus from the New Deal to the Civil Rights Movement* (New York: Oxford University Press, 2008), 65–67, 77–81, 179–181; Selig, *Americans All*, ch. 4, "Religious Education and the Teaching of Goodwill"; and Schultz, *Tri-Faith America*, 64–67.

46 PHS, RG 18 Box 61 Folder 1.

47 Ibid.

48 Ibid.

49 PHS, RG 18 Box 61 Folder 4.

CHAPTER 4. THE CHURCH IN THE WORLD

1 On the race riots in Detroit and Harlem and the more general problems of adjustment to changing conditions in urban centers during the war years, see John Patrick Diggins, *The Proud Decades: America in War and Peace, 1941–1960* (New York: W. W. Norton & Company, 1989), 27–34; and David M. Kennedy, *Freedom from Fear: The American People in Depression and War, 1929–1945* (New York: Oxford University Press, 1999), 768–771.

2 PHS, RG 18 Box 58 Folder 6.

3 Ibid. Although Haynes continued to emphasize the importance of contacts, in this context he seemed to grant prior conditioning a more explicit role in forming persons and their prejudices. There is also a sense in which he does not grant contacts the power to alter habits in the way that he did in previous essays. If indeed these contacts lead to misunderstanding and perhaps violence, then what is it about contacts that alter previously formed patterns? Where and in what context were they formed? It appears that Haynes's views were undergoing some

change in terms of how contacts affect attitudes and conditioning and the locus of these prior experiences that shaped them.

4 PHS, RG 18 Box 58 Folder 6.
5 Ibid.
6 Ibid.
7 Ibid.
8 PHS, RG 18 Box 59 Folder 5.
9 PHS, RG 18 Box 59 Folder 5.
10 Ibid.
11 PHS, RG 18 Box 59 Folder 1.
12 PHS, RG 18 Box 59 Folder 5.
13 Ibid.
14 PHS, RG 18 Box 59 Folder 1.
15 Ibid.
16 Ibid.
17 PHS, RG 18 Box 56 Folder 5.
18 PHS, RG 18 Box 1 Folder 2.
19 For a sound analysis of this problem of defining the FCC's mission and role, see Schneider, "Voice of Many Waters," in Hutchison, *Between the Times*, 105–107.
20 PHS, RG 18 Box 56 Folder 4.
21 Ibid.
22 Ibid.
23 Hutchison, *The Modernist Impulse in American Protestantism*, 2. For another helpful reflection on the aims and consequences of liberal Protestant efforts at social reform, see Richard Wightman Fox, "The Culture of Liberal Protestant Progressivism, 1875–1925," *Journal of Interdisciplinary History* 23, no. 3 (Winter 1993), 639–660.
24 William G. McLoughlin, *Revivals, Awakenings, and Reform: An Essay on Religion and Social Change in America, 1607–1977* (Chicago: University of Chicago Press, 1978), 156.
25 Ibid., 162.
26 Walter Rauschenbusch, *Christianity and the Social Crisis* (Louisville, KY: Westminster/John Knox Press, 1991 [1907]), 349.
27 Ibid., 349–350.
28 PHS, RG 18 Box 60 Folder 19.
29 Ibid.
30 PHS, RG 18 Box 59 Folder 8. For more on Van Kleeck, who had grown increasingly supportive of Communism by the early 1930s, see *American National Biography*, vol. 22 (New York: Oxford University Press, 1999), 224–226.
31 Ibid.
32 PHS, PG 18 Box 57 Folder 9.
33 Ibid.

34 Ibid.

35 PHS, RG 18 Box 57 Folder 9.

CHAPTER 5. ECUMENICAL PROTESTANTISM AND THE LIMITS OF RACIAL REFORM

1 PHS, RG 18 Box 56 Folder 7.

2 Ibid.

3 See Matthew Pratt Guterl, *The Color of Race in America, 1900–1940* (Cambridge, MA: Harvard University Press, 2001), especially 1–27. Guterl regards the late 1920s and early 1930s as crucial for the hardening of racial categories and an almost exclusive focus on the "race problem" as black and white. As I indicate in this chapter, the FCC from the early 1920s had already begun thinking about other minority groups besides African Americans, even though the bulk of its resources were devoted to African Americans and the particular problems they faced, especially in the South. Even so, there was constant discussion about the nature of race and "race relations," and never a settled notion that it was exclusively black and white.

4 See Diana Selig, *Americans All: The Cultural Gifts Movement* (Cambridge, MA: Harvard University Press, 2008).

5 On this point, see David A. Hollinger, *Postethnic America: Beyond Multiculturalism* (New York: Basic Books, 1995), 91–95.

6 Haynes, *Trend of the Races*, 69, 72. On the persistence of romantic racialism in the 1920s, see Evans, *Burden of Black Religion*, ch. 5. For the significance of the Harmon Foundation in black artistic endeavors, see Gary A. Reynolds and Beryl J. Wright, eds, *Against the Odds: African Americans and the Harmon Foundation* (Newark, NJ: Newark Museum Assn., 1989).

7 See Mary Ann Calo, *Distinction and Denial: Race, Nation, and the Critical Construction of the African American Artist, 1920–1940* (Ann Arbor: University of Michigan Press, 2007), 75–76; and Erma Meadows Mallow, "African American Visual Artists and the Harmon Foundation," diss., Columbia University Teachers College, 1991, 73.

8 *Trend of the Races*, 86.

9 Calo, *Distinction and Denial*, 75.

10 Evans, *Burden of Black Religion*, 193.

11 Mallow, "African American Visual Artists," 73.

12 Calo, *Distinction and Denial*, 76–77. Yet, despite Haynes's desire to display this art in "positive" contexts, in local communities white elites controlled the location and setting of these exhibits, often reinforcing the racial conventions of the community, such as a segregated showing in Atlanta in 1929. See Mallow, "African American Visual Artists," 102–109.

13 Calo, *Distinction and Denial*, 74.

14 Haynes expressed weariness about lengthy discussions of "the race problem" and preferred action, exhibitions, and ritual practices that helped to shape and

condition emotions through encounters and mutual projects. See his *Trend of the Races*, 179.

15 PHS, RG 18 Box 59 Folder 8. On the work of the American Friends Service Committee, see Allan W. Austin, *Quaker Brotherhood: Interracial Activism and the American Friends Service Committee, 1917–1950* (Urbana: University of Illinois Press, 2012). As Austin notes, though Quakers began interracial work in the mid-1920s and intimated support for diversity, most of their own institutions remained segregated.

16 PHS, RG 18 Box 56 Folder 4.

17 Desmond King, *Immigration, Race, and the Origins of the Diverse Democracy* (Cambridge, MA: Harvard University Press, 2000), 200–201. See also Matthew Frye Jacobson, *Whiteness of a Different Color: European Immigrants and the Alchemy of Race* (Cambridge, MA: Harvard University Press, 1999).

18 PHS, RG 18 Box 56 Folder 20.

19 For more on Haynes and Mays, see David Wills, "An Enduring Distance: Black Americans and the Establishment," in Hutchison, *Between the Times*, 172–182.

20 PHS, RG 18 Box 56 Folder 5.

21 On the point about the FCC in comparison with other groups equal to its size, see Hollinger, "After Cloven Tongues of Fire: Ecumenical Protestantism and the Modern Encounter with Diversity," 31.

22 PHS, RG 18 Box 56 Folder 13.

23 PHS, RG 18 Box 58 Folder 4.

24 Ibid.

25 Ibid.

26 Ibid.

27 PHS, RG 18 Box 56 Folder 6.

28 PHS, RG 18 Box 56 Folder 12.

29 Ibid.

30 On this point, see Findlay, *Church People in the Struggle*, 30.

31 PHS, RG 18 Box 56 Folder 4.

32 Ibid.

33 PHS, RG 18 Box 54 Folder 4.

34 PHS, RG 18 Box 56 Folder 5.

35 PHS, RG 18 Box 57 Folder 14.

36 Ibid.

37 For a reprint and good introduction to *Plessy*, see Thomas, *Plessy v. Ferguson: A Brief History with Documents*.

38 PHS, RG 18 Box 57 Folder 14.

39 Ibid.

40 Ibid.

41 Ibid.

42 Ibid.

43 Ibid.

44 Hollinger, "After Cloven Tongues of Fire: Ecumenical Protestantism and the Modern Encounter with Diversity," 23.

45 Historical judgments about shortcomings are notoriously difficult, especially when one considers the structural obstacles faced by even the gradualist and reformist projects of the FCC. However, one can only speak from one's own vantage point and in hindsight, as problematic as that might be in trying to create an accurate historical narrative that does not impose simplistically normative judgments from one's contemporary context.

46 PHS, RG 18 Box 56 Folder 1.

47 PHS, RG 18 Box 80 Folder 2.

48 Ibid.

49 For this provocative and, in my view, mostly plausible interpretation, see Donald G. Mathews, "Lynching is Part of the Religion of Our People: Faith in the Christian South," in Beth Barton Schweiger and Donald G. Mathews, eds., *Religion in the American South: Protestants and Others in History and Culture* (Chapel Hill: University of North Carolina Press, 2004), 153–194.

50 Amy Louise Wood, *Lynching and Spectacle: Witnessing Racial Violence in America, 1890–1940* (Chapel Hill: University of North Carolina Press, 2009), 49.

51 PHS, RG 18 Box 59 Folder 20.

52 Gunnar Myrdal, *An American Dilemma: The Negro Problem and Modern Democracy*, vol 1 (New Brunswick, NJ: Transaction Publishers, 2002 [1944]), 587.

53 Fay Botham, *Almighty God Created the Races: Christianity, Interracial Marriage, & American Law* (Chapel Hill: University of North Carolina Press, 2009), 131–135.

54 Jane Dailey, "Sex, Segregation, and the Sacred after *Brown*," 122.

55 Ibid., 127–129.

56 PHS, RG 18 Box 57 Folder 14.

57 Ibid.

58 On the role of the FCC and ecumenical leaders more generally in the articulation of human rights in the United Nations, see John S. Nurser, *For All Peoples and All Nations: The Ecumenical Church and Human Rights* (Washington, DC: Georgetown University Press, 2005).

59 Savage, *Your Spirits Walk Beside Us*, 211–212.

60 For more on how this process evolved, see Botham, *Almighty God Created the Races*.

61 One early study of the Russell Sage Foundation (which was a major funder of the Department and thus an important source of information, given the need for the FCC's Department of Race Relations to formulate its purpose as a condition of getting the grant) tried to capture the central mission and duties of the Department of Race Relations, and it overlapped in significant ways with Haynes's internal assessment. The study noted that the Department's purpose was to promote local interracial committees and stimulate churches' interest in race relations. The study

saw the Department as a "clearinghouse for information"; the organizer of Race Relations Sundays; a protestor against mob violence; and an organization that sought to "further the equitable provision for the Negro in education, housing, recreation, and medical care, and fair opportunities for employment." John M. Glenn, Lilian Brandt, and F. Emerson Andrews, *Russell Sage Foundation, 1907–1946*, vol. 2 (New York: Russell Sage Foundation, 1947), 473.

62 PHS, RG 18 Box 61 Folder 14.

63 For more on this point, see W. Clark Gilpin, *A Preface to Theology* (Chicago: University of Chicago Press, 1996), 97–100.

64 David L. Chappell, *Prophetic Religion and the Death of Jim Crow* (Chapel Hill: University of North Carolina Press, 2004), 11.

65 I was helped by Grant Wacker's *Heaven Below: Early Pentecostals and American Culture* (Cambridge, MA: Harvard University Press, 2001), ch. 5, in teasing out the constituent cultural and theological features of spiritual cosmos. This is part of my attempt to get scholars to take seriously the theological world and religious practices of liberal and ecumenical Protestants in the way that they have been all too willing to do among working class religious groups like early Pentecostals, who practiced and advocated a more supernaturalistic Christianity.

66 Jill K. Gill, *Embattled Ecumenism: The National Council of Churches, the Vietnam War, and the Trial of the Protestant Left* (Dekalb: Northern Illinois University Press, 2011), 18.

CONCLUSION: LEGACIES OF LIBERAL PROTESTANTISM AND RACE

1 Findlay, *Church People in the Struggle*, 3. Similar to criticisms that had been leveled at the FCC, but even more virulent during the Civil Rights movement, opposition to the NCC was harsh in the South. Carolyn Renee Dupont argues that such animus was at its harshest in Mississippi in 1961, 1962, and 1964, but she also points to 1963 as the year when the NCC moved to a more active stance for racial justice, and beyond "simple pronouncements that affirmed the principle of racial equality." See Dupont, *Mississippi Praying: Southern White Evangelicals and the Civil Rights Movement, 1945–1975* (New York: New York University Press, 2013), 133.

2 See Dailey, "Sex, Segregation, and the Sacred after *Brown*," 120–122. Dailey writes that, even for many scholars, "true Christianity" has become synonymous with this vision of Christianity, and with Martin Luther King, Jr.'s model of the beloved community.

3 James F. Burks, "Integration or Segregation" (May 30, 1954), in Dailey, *The Age of Jim Crow*, 280.

4 Reinhold Niebuhr, *Moral Man and Immoral Society: A Study in Ethics and Politics* (New York: Charles Scribner's Sons, 1960 [1932]), 3.

5 Rachel Davis-DuBois, *Get Together Americans: Friendly Approaches to Racial and Cultural Conflicts through the Neighborhood-Home Festival* (New York: Harper & Brothers, 1943), 2–3.

6 For a radical, activist version of Christian nonviolence (in contrast with the FCC's nonviolent and conciliatory tactics) that emphasized economic equality and racial justice, and involved such groups as the Fellowship of Reconciliation and a few individuals who had close relationships to ecumenical Protestantism, see Kip Kosek, *Acts of Conscience: Christian Non-Violence and Modern American Democracy* (New York: Columbia University Press, 2011).

7 J. Russell Hawkins, *The Bible Told Them So: How Southern Evangelicals Fought to Preserve White Supremacy* (New York: Oxford University Press, 2021), 7–8.

8 See Jane Dailey, *White Fright: The Sexual Panic at the Heart of American's Racist History* (New York: Basic Books, 2020), 165. Dailey details the ways in which white Christian segregationists linked brotherhood to Communism, one world government, and racial integration, which meant for them a rebellion against the very laws of God.

9 For more on the criticism of the FCC and its successor, the NCC, by the religious and political Right, see Markku Ruotsila, "'Russia's Most Effective Fifth Column': Cold War Perceptions of Un-Americanism in US Churches," *Journal of American Studies* 47, no. 4 (2013), 1019–1041.

10 Findlay, *Church People in the Struggle*, 30.

INDEX

ABOUT THE AUTHOR

Curtis J. Evans is Associate Professor of American Religions and the History of Christianity at the University of Chicago Divinity School. He is the author of *The Burden of Black Religion*. He is a scholar of American religious history, focusing on race and religion, Christianity and slavery in the US, and religion and social change. He is a past recipient of the Charles Warren Center Faculty Fellowship, and was a Henry Luce III Fellow in Theology. He has taught courses on the Social Gospel, evangelicals and race, religion and race in the US in the twentieth century, American religion since the Civil War, and the religious and social thought of Martin Luther King, Jr.